PRAISE FOR TRAVIS WINFIELD

The military prepares you for the battlefield but leaves you financially unprepared. Military Money and MORE is the field manual you were never issued. In this no-bull$#!t guide, Navy veteran Travis Winfield provides a mission-ready plan to shift from a consumer to an investor. Learn to acquire assets and leverage your most powerful, underutilized benefit: the VA Home Loan. Discover how to turn every PCS move into a strategic, wealth-building opportunity that can secure your family's future. If you're ready to execute the mission for your financial independence, these are your new orders.

WILL GRIMES, CEO & CO-FOUNDER, MILE HIGH PROPERTY BROTHERS; USMC VETERAN

From my time serving as Master Chief Petty Officer of the Coast Guard, I saw how financial problems create and exacerbate many other work/life issues. In this book, Travis Winfield helps us chart a course to not just financial security but success in life. He draws from his own experience to provide easy-to-understand and practical advice. Travis has an amazing way of making difficult decisions easier through his NO BS and candid direction. This is not a once-and-done book—you will use this information for the rest of your life.

JASON VANDERHADEN, 13TH MASTER CHIEF PETTY OFFICER OF THE COAST GUARD, USCG RETIRED

Are you the ONE? The ONE who can ensure your family's future financial success? You work hard for your money—Travis works to invest life lessons and proper planning into you through Military Money and MORE. This book is an investment in you and your future, so your money can work for you. As a retiree after 30 years, I can tell you this quick and easy knowledge builder will help you relax a great deal in your future. Start today with this amazing tool, get to work, and sharpen your skills to grow a successful and wealthy future. It begins with the investment in yourself and this book, but it's your commitment to action that will make the difference. Be the ONE.

SCOTT A. BENNING, AUTHOR OF *POWER OF POSITIVE LEADERSHIP*; FLEET MASTER CHIEF, USN RETIRED

Military Money and MORE is more than just a financial guide—it's a manual for every service member who wants to take control of their financial future. Drawing from personal challenges and victories, Travis shares a deeply personal and relatable journey that makes the principles of budgeting, saving, investing, and home buying understandable and actionable. An honest, practical book that turns personal experience into a powerful guide for financial freedom.

ERIC BENKEN, 12TH CHIEF MASTER SERGEANT OF THE AIR FORCE, USAF RETIRED

Military Money and MORE cuts through the noise with raw honesty and hard-earned wisdom. Travis Winfield delivers the kind of straight talk on financial readiness that every service member deserves but rarely gets. This is the guide I wish I had early in my career and one every military leader should read and hand to their people.

MIKE STEVENS, 13TH MASTER CHIEF PETTY OFFICER OF THE NAVY; CEO, NAVY LEAGUE OF THE UNITED STATES; USN RETIRED

Travis Winfield has hit the bullseye of the issue experienced by virtually every young warrior and civilian in our country. That is, 'how to manage their money and build wealth.' His incredibly accurate assessment of what drives the problems, illustrated with his personal stumbles with finances as a young Sailor, delivers the ah-ha! moment to the reader with the realization they are not alone in making the inevitable money mistakes we all make. Not only does he point out the problems, but he goes the extra mile to educate the reader with ways to dig out of their problem followed by ways to actually become financially sound by building wealth for life. Every parent and leader of those navigating their personal financial journey should use this very easy read and incredibly useful book.

JIM HERDT, 9TH MASTER CHIEF PETTY OFFICER OF THE NAVY, CEO/CFO HERDT CONSULTING, USN RETIRED

Financial freedom isn't just about escaping the 9 to 5—it's about reclaiming your time, your purpose, and your ability to serve others from a position of strength. This book isn't theory—it's a weapon for those ready to fight for their future.

BUDDY RUSHING, CEO/FOUNDER, WHITE FEATHER INVESTMENTS, USMC VETERAN

MILITARY MONEY & MORE

TRAVIS WINFIELD

Military Money and MORE: The No Bull$#!T Guide to Financial Freedom

ISBNs
- Paperback: 979-8-9931599-1-1
- Hardcover: 979-8-9931599-2-8

Published by TWG Inc.

This book is for educational purposes only. It is not intended to provide financial, legal, or investment advice. Readers should consult qualified professionals regarding their personal financial situation.

For resources and updates, visit:
www.militaryoperatedrealestate.com
www.traviswinfield.com

Printed in the United States of America

CONTENTS

FOREWORD

BY LARRY BROUGHTON

You stand at a crossroads. Your military service forged your discipline, resilience, and a mission-driven mindset, but now you face a new battlefield: the pursuit of financial freedom. Travis Winfield's *Military, Money, and MORE* is your guide, your battle plan, your blueprint to conquer this foreign terrain. I've walked this path as a best-selling author, an entrepreneur and CEO who built enterprises from the ground up, and a veteran who knows the weight of sacrifice. Let me tell you: Travis's story and strategies resonate because they're real, hard-earned, and built for you.

Picture this: a young Sailor, fresh from enlistment, clutching a paycheck that feels like freedom. He buys a flashy car, maxes out credit cards, and assumes the future will sort itself out. That was Travis once, and maybe it's been you. He racked up $40,000 in debt, lived paycheck to paycheck, and thought hustle alone would save him. But he learned a truth that changed everything: financial success isn't about how much you earn—it's about how you manage and grow it. By 2009, stationed in Italy, Travis bought his second home in California using his VA Home Loan, a move that sparked his journey to wealth through real estate and entrepreneurship. Today, he owns multiple properties, runs thriving businesses, and mentors others to do the same. His story proves you can start from nothing, break the multi-generational curse of poverty, and build a legacy.

Why does this matter to you? Because the military gave you unique tools: structure, a sense of mission, focus, benefits like the VA Home Loan and Thrift Savings Plan, that most civilians can only dream of. Yet, as Travis notes, only 12% of the 16 million veterans in the U.S. have used their VA Home Loan. Why? Too many lack the financial foundation to qualify. This powerful book tackles that root cause head-on, offering clear steps to master budgeting, crush debt, build credit, and invest smartly. It's not just about buying a home; it's about creating wealth that lasts generations.

Let's talk numbers. Over 60% of service members live paycheck to paycheck, according to the National Foundation for Credit Counseling. Nearly one-third face food insecurity during their careers, per a 2021 Department of Defense study. These aren't abstract stats, they're your brother and sister vets, struggling not because they lack intelligence or income, but because they lack know-how. Travis flips that script. He shares how he turned his BAH into equity by buying properties at each duty station, how he used whole life insurance to fund businesses, and how he leveraged SkillBridge to transition smoothly. You can do this, too. Start small: save $50 per paycheck, invest $200 a month in a Roth IRA, buy a duplex and rent out half. Small moves compound into big wins.

What's holding you back? If you're like most others, it's the deadly combination of believing the ugly myth that you need a big salary to build wealth, and the fear of failure. The truth is, I've seen fear among military comrades and peers in the boardrooms, but the greatest risk is inaction. Travis echoes this, drawing from Robert Kiyosaki's *Rich Dad, Poor Dad*: "It's not how much money you make, it's what you do with it." Kiyosaki's lesson reshaped Travis's mindset, pushing him to buy assets, not liabilities. When I started my first company, I had no capital, just a vision and grit. I leaned on mentors, took calculated risks, and learned from every setback. You have that same grit deep inside of you. Use it. Never forget, tenacity eats talent for lunch!

This book isn't theory, it's a how-to manual. Travis lays out actionable steps: track every dollar, build an emergency fund, pay off high-interest debt first, max out your TSP, buy real estate at every PCS. He shares his mistakes, like blowing bonuses on lifestyle inflation, so you don't repeat them. He also highlights resources like SBA loans, Boots to Business training, and veteran networking groups. Take Will Rivera, an Army veteran who used an SBA loan to launch Running Soles, a thriving shoe store, or Mitch Goodwin, who grew a $12 million construction firm with VBOC guidance. These veterans didn't have silver spoons; they had plans and persistence. You can follow their lead.

What's your vision? A debt-free home? A business that lets you call the shots? A retirement where you choose how to spend your days? Travis's story shows it's possible. Growing up, he slept on a foam mattress, made his own salad dressing to save money, and faced a turning point when caught shoplifting as a teen. A judge's second chance via the Pathfinders program taught him accountability, setting him on a path to twenty-four years in the Navy and a life of impact. His journey from struggle to success mirrors what you can achieve with focus and action.

My own journey has taught me that a key component of leadership is taking responsibility for your future. In the military, you planned missions with precision and 5 Point Contingency Plans; apply that to your finances. Open a brokerage account today. Meet with a fiduciary advisor tomorrow. Explore a VA loan next week. Every step moves you closer to freedom. As John F. Kennedy, a Navy veteran, once said, *"Efforts and courage are not enough without purpose and direction."* This book gives you both.

You served your country in uniform. Now, serve yourself and your family by building a future where money is a tool, not a burden. Travis's blueprint works because it's rooted in experience, not hype. Read this book. Act on its lessons. Join the MORE community to connect with veterans who've walked this path. Your mission starts now. Will you answer the call?

Dream big, start small, move fast! Now, go get 'em!

BIO: ***Larry Broughton is a former US Army Green Beret, best-selling author, award-winning entrepreneur & CEO, keynote speaker, and leadership mentor. @LarryBroughton www.LarryBroughton.com***

INTRODUCTION: MILITARY, MONEY, AND MORE

The military teaches discipline, strategy, and resilience, but what it doesn't always teach is financial literacy. For many service members, transitioning from active duty to civilian life is a battlefield of its own, filled with financial uncertainty, career shifts, and the overwhelming challenge of building wealth. I know this struggle firsthand.

When I first enlisted in the Navy in 1992, financial freedom wasn't even a concept I considered. Like many service members, I lived paycheck to paycheck, focused on my mission and my duties, and assumed that financial stability would somehow fall into place later. I made the same mistakes so many of my brothers and sisters in uniform made: overspending, under-saving, and failing to leverage the benefits I had earned through service. I lacked resources, but more importantly, I lacked the knowledge to use what was available to me.

It wasn't until years into my military career that I had an awakening. I realized that financial success wasn't about how much money you make; it was about how well you manage and grow what you have. I started learning everything I could about money, credit, investing, and homeownership. Eventually, I leveraged my **VA Home Loan** to purchase my first home, and from there, I built wealth through real estate, entrepreneurship, and smart financial strategies. I have owned multiple properties, run a successful real estate business, and mentored veterans and active-duty service members on how to escape financial uncertainty and build lasting wealth.

But here's the problem: out of the **19 million veterans and service members** in our country, **only about 12%** have ever used their VA home loan benefits. That means roughly **88% of eligible vets** aren't taking advantage of what could be the single most powerful financial tool in their benefit package. One major reason is that nearly **35% of post-9/11 veterans** face housing cost burdens—struggling to afford homeownership even when working full-time.

This is the real issue we need to solve. Too many people in real estate focus only on the 12% who are already financially qualified, teaching them about VA Home Loans and homeownership benefits. But that's treating the symptom, not the disease. If we want to truly impact the lives of military families, we must address the root cause: financial illiteracy. Without a strong financial foundation, veterans and service members will continue to struggle, regardless of the benefits available to them.

That's why I wrote *Military, Money, and MORE*: to equip veterans, active-duty military, and their families with the knowledge and tools they need to achieve financial success. This book isn't just about using your VA Home Loan; it's about understanding money, building wealth, and creating a legacy.

The Military, Money, and MORE Blueprint

In this book, I will guide you through the essential financial strategies that every military family needs to know, including:

Budgeting & Debt Management – How to stop living paycheck to paycheck and take control of your money.

Credit Mastery – How to build and maintain a strong credit score (a key factor in homeownership).

Leveraging Military Benefits – Understanding the VA Home Loan, Thrift Savings Plan (TSP), and other wealth-building opportunities.

Real Estate Investing – How to use your VA Home Loan strategically to build long-term wealth.

Transitioning to Civilian Financial Success – Planning for life after the military, from business ownership to passive income.

It's Time to Take Action

This isn't about luck or background, it's about strategy and execution. I went from being an enlisted service member with no financial knowledge to building a successful business and real estate portfolio. If I can do it, so can you. Homeownership, financial freedom, or success is not an entitlement, you have to earn it. And just like in the military, the path to victory starts with a plan, discipline, and execution.

Let's begin the mission!

From Humble Beginnings to Financial Freedom

I wasn't born into wealth. I wasn't handed a roadmap to success. In fact, for much of my early life, I was just trying to figure out how to survive. Growing up as an only child, I split my time between two very different but equally challenging worlds. During the week, I lived with my mom in Richmond, Virginia, where she worked tirelessly to provide for us. She always made sure we had a roof over our heads and food on the table, but we struggled. When we moved to the West End of Richmond, it was a wealthier area, but we were far from affluent. In fact, I was probably one of the poorest kids in my high school.

I got teased a lot for wearing hand-me-down clothes, and while my classmates had name-brand food, I learned how to make my own Thousand Island dressing with mayonnaise, ketchup, and relish because we couldn't afford the real thing. I remember moving into an apartment with my mom, but we couldn't afford much furniture. For years, I didn't even have my own bed. Instead, I slept on a foam egg crate mattress on the floor, with my toys scattered around because I didn't have a dresser.

Despite these challenges, my mom never gave up. She worked herself to exhaustion to keep us afloat, but as soon as I was old enough to stay home alone, I became a latchkey kid. That meant long days by myself, figuring out how to navigate life without much guidance. It was lonely, but it also taught me independence.

Then there were the weekends with my dad, where life was a different kind of struggle. He lived in a rough neighborhood, and his apartment got broken into multiple times a year. I remember going to visit him, knowing that at any moment, our stuff could be stolen or our home violated. It wasn't the safest environment, but it was part of my reality.

Despite their financial struggles, both my parents did their absolute best. And even though money was tight, we made memories. I remember getting a silver dollar for my birthday, and instead of keeping it, I used it to take my mom to a Sunday matinee for fifty cents. To this day, that remains one of my favorite childhood memories—not because of the movie, but because of what it symbolized: making the most out of what we had.

From Rebellion to Realization

I wasn't always the disciplined, mission-driven leader I am today. In fact, I spent much of my early years doing everything possible to go against the grain. My mom became my first mentor. She hustled, working in sales and traveling across the state, often taking me along on her business calls. Riding with her, I learned more about business and sales than I realized at the time.

Despite her efforts, I was a painfully shy and nerdy kid. The thick-rimmed glasses, held together by tape, didn't help. In the seventh grade, I finally found a group of friends who accepted me, but they weren't exactly the best influences. We were what they called back then "headbangers," a bunch of mullet-wearing, heavy metal-loving kids who spent our time sneaking out, experimenting with drugs, stealing, and getting into trouble.

By the eighth grade, I was fully immersed into that lifestyle. I wasn't necessarily a bad kid, I just had no direction. I started mouthing off to teachers, skipping class, and spending half the year in in-school suspension. I developed a kleptomania problem, not stealing from people but from stores, believing it didn't really hurt anyone. My friends and I became so comfortable with it that we'd walk right out of stores with whatever we wanted. I couldn't afford those things, so I just took them. Until one day, it all came crashing down.

On what felt like a routine shoplifting run at the mall, my friends and I were caught red-handed, paraded through the store in handcuffs, and handed over to the police. That moment should have been humiliating, but at the time, I barely cared. It wasn't until I stood in front of a judge that I realized I had reached a turning point.

Instead of giving me a harsh sentence, the judge offered me a second chance: a six-month program called Pathfinders that would erase my record if I successfully completed it. That program changed my life. It taught me discipline, accountability, and the power of making better choices. It made me realize I had the potential to do so much more with my life.

Finding Focus & Direction

Despite my less than stellar past, I still had a strong work ethic, but lacked focus. I didn't know what my true calling was. I bounced between jobs, always working hard but never finding the right path. That all changed when I met Colonel Upchurch, a retired Marine Corps fighter pilot who ran a vocational aviation training program at my high school. He was a true leader—the kind of man who commanded respect just by walking into a room.

Under his mentorship, I went from an unfocused teenager with a 2.1 GPA to one of the top students in my school with a 3.6 GPA. He showed me what discipline, responsibility, and leadership looked like. That's when I made the decision to join the military.

The Navy gave me structure, opportunity, and the ability to try new things. While I served for twenty-four years, I was able to change jobs every three years, keeping things fresh and challenging. The military allowed me to explore different career paths, develop my leadership skills, and learn how to adapt to new challenges.

Learning the Value of Hard Work

By the time I turned fourteen, I was ready to take control of my own financial situation. In Virginia, fourteen was the earliest age you could legally work, so I wasted no time: the day I turned fourteen, I got my worker's permit and landed my first job at McDonald's.

But for me, working wasn't just about earning a little spending money. It became a way of life. Between the ages of fourteen and nineteen, I worked seventeen different jobs, trying to figure out what I was good at and searching for the right path. I worked everywhere—from fast food to retail, to gas stations, from working in warehouses to delivering pizzas. I never stopped hustling.

Even after I joined the military, my work ethic never changed. While many service members focused solely on their Navy careers, I was always working two or three jobs at a time. I did everything from selling security systems to working at Best Buy; yes, even as a Senior Chief Petty Officer in the Navy, I worked at Best Buy just to provide for my family. It wasn't because we had to; we made the decision early on that my wife would stay home to raise our kids, and I would be the sole provider. That commitment drove me to always find ways to earn more, save more, and build a better future for our family.

The Turning Point: From Military to Money Mastery

In 2009, while stationed in Italy, I made one of the most important financial decisions of my life: I purchased my second home in California using my VA Home Loan. My real estate agent was Derek Barksdale, an active-duty service member who went out of his way to help me, even using his own leave to pick me up at the airport for house hunting.

That experience changed everything. I saw firsthand how homeownership could transform a military family's future. But I also saw how many service members never took advantage of their benefits because they simply weren't financially prepared. That's when it clicked—financial literacy is the foundation of everything. From that moment on, I became obsessed with helping veterans and military families break free from financial struggle.

Why I Wrote This Book

Too many people in the real estate industry focus only on selling to the 12%—the veterans who are already financially stable enough to qualify for a mortgage. But that's treating the symptom, not the disease. If we want to change the narrative for military families, we have to address the root cause—financial literacy. That's why I wrote *Military Money & MORE*—not just to talk about VA Home Loans, but to give veterans and military families a real plan for financial success.

In this book, I will teach you:

How to break free from living paycheck to paycheck

How to build and maintain strong credit

How to budget and eliminate debt

How to leverage military benefits for financial growth

How to use real estate to create long-term wealth

I've lived on both sides of the financial struggle. I know what it's like to sleep on a foam mattress on the floor. I also know what it's like to own multiple properties, run businesses, and build wealth. And now, I want to help you do the same. This isn't about luck; it's about having the right plan, the right mindset, and the right strategy. At the end of each chapter, I have offered you the space to jot down those ideas, observations, questions, or whatever else comes to mind so that at the end of this book, you will have that list of things that will help you further explore, refine, and develop the right plan, mindset, and strategy for wherever you find yourself in your career.

Disclaimer: I am not a financial advisor or a tax professional! Everything I provide here is based on my personal experience and knowledge. I highly encourage you to consult a **fiduciary** financial advisor, and I emphasize **fiduciary** because that means they are **legally obligated** to make investment decisions in your best interest rather than lining their own pockets. Too many so-called "financial advisors" are really just glorified salespeople pushing high-fee products that benefit them more than you. **Don't fall into that trap.**

Want to learn more? **LET'S GET TO WORK!**

ONE
THE FINANCIAL BATTLEFIELD FOR MILITARY FAMILIES

LET'S go deeper into the biggest challenge most service members face, the military instills discipline, resilience, and a mission-first mindset, but there's one critical area where many service members are thrown to the wolves with zero guidance: financial literacy. We train for combat, deployments, and field exercises. We can assemble a rifle blindfolded, but ask the average service member about compound interest, credit utilization, or how to read a mortgage statement, and you'll get a blank stare and a response like, *"Uh... is that in the Bluejackets' Manual?"*

Let's be real, money management isn't part of boot camp, and there sure as hell isn't a PowerPoint briefing on how to avoid buying a Mustang at 23% interest after you reenlist (which, by the way, is basically a military rite of passage at this point). I've seen it happen: a young service member gets their first real paycheck, get stars in their eyes, and suddenly they're financing a car that costs more than their annual salary. If you think I'm exaggerating, take a walk through any military base parking lot and count the number of tricked-out sports cars with temporary plates.

We prepare for every mission with precision. We plan logistics, secure the perimeter, and always have a contingency plan in case things go sideways. But when it comes to personal finances, most of us are running blind, hoping that "future me" will magically figure it all out. Spoiler alert: future you is just as clueless if you don't get your finances squared away now.

And that's a dangerous battlefield to navigate without the right tools. One wrong move, signing a terrible loan, maxing out a credit card, or not investing early; and you could be stuck in financial quicksand for years. I learned this the hard way when I racked up $40,000 in credit card debt, thinking I was just "managing" my money like an adult. Turns out that paying the minimum payment doesn't make your debt disappear; it just makes you a slave to high interest rates for eternity.

So, here's the deal: if the military trained us in personal finance the way it trained us in combat skills, we'd all be rich. But since that's not happening anytime soon, it's up to us to learn the strategies, build wealth, and make sure we're financially squared away, just like we would for any mission.

THE REALITY OF MILITARY FINANCES

Many people assume that military service comes with built-in financial stability, after all, we get steady paychecks, housing allowances, and healthcare benefits. On paper, it sounds like a pretty sweet deal. But here's the reality: financial hardship is more common in the military than people think, and, in many cases, it's even worse than in the civilian world. Why? Because while civilians are at least forced to face their finances head-on, many service members float through their careers without ever truly learning how to manage money.

I've witnessed it firsthand, and I've lived through it. I've made some seriously dumb financial mistakes—mistakes that made me question my life choices more than a 20-mile ruck march in full gear. And the worst part? I wasn't alone. The numbers don't lie:

- **Over 60% of service members live paycheck to paycheck** (National Foundation for Credit Counseling). That means more than half of us are counting down the days until payday like it's Christmas morning, just to keep the lights on.
- **27% of military families have more than $10,000 in credit card debt** (Military Family Advisory Network). I was one of them. As I mentioned before, I had over $40,000 in debt and trust me, it wasn't because I was out there making high-value investments.
- **Nearly one-third of service members experience food insecurity at some point during their careers** (Department of Defense study, 2021). I personally know military families who wait in line at food banks because their entire paycheck goes toward rent, car payments, and debt.
- **More than 50% of veterans do not feel financially prepared for civilian life after separation** (Pew Research Center). I get it: transitioning out of the military without a financial plan feels like jumping out of a plane without a parachute.

These numbers don't just represent money problems; they represent stress, uncertainty, and missed opportunities. They mean families arguing over bills, service members taking out payday loans at 400% interest just to make it to the next paycheck, and veterans struggling to make ends meet after separation.

Here's the thing: most financial struggles in the military aren't because of a lack of income; they're because of a lack of financial education. And that's not our fault. Nowhere in boot camp or professional development courses does anyone sit down and say, *"Alright, listen up! Here's how to budget, invest, and build wealth so you're not broke when you get out!"* Nope. Instead, we're left to figure it out the hard way.

And let's be real: if there's one thing the military excels at, it's keeping you just comfortable enough to survive, but never comfortable enough to thrive. You get paid just enough to make it to the next paycheck, just enough to qualify for a car loan (at an outrageous interest rate), and just enough to keep you reliant on that steady government income, making the thought of separating absolutely terrifying.

The good news? You can break out of that cycle. You can go from barely scraping by to building real wealth, but first, you have to understand the game that's being played around you. And that's exactly what we're going to tackle in this book. Because the military may not teach you financial literacy, but I sure as hell will.

THE PROBLEM WITH MILITARY MONEY MANAGEMENT

So, why do so many service members struggle financially? Simple: We were never taught how to handle money.

The military does a phenomenal job of teaching us how to follow orders, prepare for battle, and function in high-stress environments. But when it comes to budgeting, investing, or even understanding how our own pay works, we're left completely in the dark.

And that's how so many of us, myself included, end up making dumb financial decisions that haunt us for years. Let's break it down.

1. Lack of Financial Education in the Primary Education System

Think back to high school. Did anyone ever sit you down and explain credit scores, compound interest, or the dangers of high-interest debt? Probably not. That's because **only seven states** in the entire U.S. **require** financial literacy courses in high school. And by the time we join the military, most of us are handed a steady paycheck for the first time in our lives, more money than we've ever had before. And guess what? We have no idea what to do with it. Instead of learning about wealth-building, we get caught in the trap of over-spending, living paycheck to paycheck, and relying on credit to cover gaps.

And the proof is in the numbers:

> *****Only 12% of eligible veterans have ever used their VA Home Loan Benefit*****

Think about that—just 12%. That means 88% of veterans never even attempted to buy a piece of land in the very country they swore to protect. That's not just a statistic, that's a red flag. But why is this happening? It's not just about financial instability; several factors contribute to why veterans aren't utilizing this powerful benefit:

Lack of Financial Readiness – Many veterans struggle with debt, low credit scores, or unstable income, making homeownership feel out of reach.

Misinformation & Myths – Some veterans believe they can only use their VA Home Loan once, that it's too complicated, or that sellers won't accept VA-backed offers—none of which are true.

Fear of Commitment – Military life means frequent moves. Some veterans hesitate to buy a home because they're afraid they'll be stuck with a property they can't sell or rent out when they PCS.

Lack of Education from Lenders & Realtors – Not all lenders and real estate agents understand the VA Home Loan's advantages. If a veteran isn't working with a VA-savvy real estate professional, they might not even realize how much they're leaving on the table.

No Clear Plan for PCS-Proofing Investments – Many veterans don't see homeownership as a long-term investment strategy. They focus on the short-term, *"I won't be here long,"* instead of thinking about how they could turn that home into a rental property after they move.

Market Conditions & Interest Rates – The state of the housing market can also influence a veteran's decision to buy. High home prices, rising interest rates, and competitive bidding wars can make homeownership seem less appealing, especially for first-time buyers. Some veterans may delay buying because they're unsure if it's the "right time" to enter the market.

The bottom line? The VA Home Loan isn't just about buying a home; it's about financial empowerment. And yet, nearly nine out of ten veterans are missing out on an opportunity that could build generational wealth. I get it. When I was a young Sailor, no one ever explained to me how the VA Home Loan worked or how it could help me build wealth. And when I finally bought my first home, I didn't even use it! Why? Because I had no idea how powerful it was. The lack of financial education isn't just a minor inconvenience; it's the difference between financial freedom and financial struggle.

2. Predatory Lending & Debt Traps

If you ever need a reminder of how clueless young service members are about money, just take a walk outside any military base. What would you see?

"EZ Military Financing! No Credit? No Problem!" (Translation: we will happily screw you over with a 25% interest rate.)

Payday lenders on every corner. (Translation: get an advance on your paycheck! Just don't read the fine print about the 400% interest.)

Furniture stores offering "No Payments for a Year!" (Translation: you'll be paying triple for that couch in five years.)

These places exist for a reason: they know we have steady paychecks, and they know we don't know any better. I've seen it happen over and over again. Some young service member fresh off their first deployment walks into a car dealership, still riding the high of that tax-free combat pay. They walk out with a brand-new Mustang, a seven-year loan at 24% interest, and a monthly payment bigger than their rent.

And guess what? Six months later, they're broke, they miss a payment, and now their shiny new car is getting repossessed faster than they can say "bad decision." These debt traps aren't accidental—they're designed to keep service members stuck in a cycle of borrowing, paying interest, and never building wealth.

3. The PCS (Permanent Change of Station) Struggle

You'd think a steady government paycheck would make military families financially stable, right? Well, let's add in the PCS factor.

The average service member moves every two to three years. That's a new state, new expenses, and a whole new financial headache every time you get orders. And while the military reimburses some moving costs, they don't cover everything. The financial burden almost always falls on the service member to figure out how to pay for:

- **Temporary housing while waiting for on-base quarters**
- **Rental deposits, security fees, and first/last month's rent**
- **Moving costs that somehow aren't reimbursed**
- **Leaving behind a house they couldn't afford to keep**

I've seen too many military families lose thousands of dollars every move, not because they weren't responsible, but because they weren't financially prepared for the PCS rollercoaster.

4. The Transition to Civilian Life

Here's where the real financial panic sets in. When you're in the military, you don't have to think about paychecks, healthcare, or retirement accounts. Everything is structured. Everything is automatic. Then, one day, you wake up, and suddenly...

No more guaranteed paycheck

Healthcare is now ridiculously expensive

Finding a civilian job isn't as easy as you thought

According to the Institute for Veterans and Military Families (IVMF), **over 60% of transitioning veterans report feeling financially unprepared for civilian life.** And I totally get it. When I was preparing to separate, I had a million questions:

- **Where's my next paycheck coming from?**
- **How much will healthcare cost?**
- **What happens to my TSP?**
- **Do I have enough saved up? (Spoiler: I didn't.)**

For so many veterans, the transition is a wake-up call, one that many aren't financially ready for.

THE BOTTOM LINE: FINANCIAL STABILITY IS A CHOICE

The military provides financial stability on paper, but let's be real, paychecks and benefits alone don't equal financial success, what you do with your money is what actually matters. I've lived the struggle. I've made the dumb mistakes. I've watched friends drown in debt while their reenlistment bonus disappeared faster than a weekend in Vegas. But I also learned how to break the cycle; how to budget, build wealth, and use the benefits we actually earned to create financial freedom. And if you're reading this, so can you. Because the reality is, military money can be your greatest weapon, or your biggest weakness. The choice is yours.

UNDERSTANDING MILITARY PAY & BENEFITS

One of the biggest advantages of military service is predictable income. Whether you're deployed, stationed stateside, or going through training, you can count on a paycheck every two weeks. Unlike civilian jobs that fluctuate based on hours worked or the economy, military pay provides a level of security that many people don't have. But just because the paycheck is predictable doesn't mean it's being managed properly. To make the most of your money, you first need to understand how military pay works.

Base Pay – The Foundation

Base pay is your primary salary as a service member, and it's determined by:

- **Rank** (Pay Grade)
- **Years of Service**

For example, in 2024:

- An **E-1 (new recruit)** earns around **$2,600 per month** before taxes
- A **Senior E-6 with ten years of service** makes about **$4,800 per month** before taxes
- An **O-3 (mid-level officer)** with six years of service earns around **$7,500 per month**

This is just the starting point; military compensation goes beyond base pay, and understanding the full range of benefits can help you maximize your income.

BASIC ALLOWANCE FOR HOUSING (BAH) – FREEING UP YOUR PAYCHECK

BAH is one of the most powerful benefits service members receive. It provides tax-free money to cover housing costs, whether you rent or own a home.

- BAH varies by rank, duty station, and dependent status
- A single E-4 stationed in San Diego receives around **$3,000** per month in BAH, while an E-4 stationed in Missouri may receive **$1,500** per month
- Those living on base don't see BAH in their paycheck, but their housing is covered

Many service members miss the opportunity to leverage their BAH by purchasing a home instead of renting. With the VA Home Loan, service members can buy a house with zero down, but most never take advantage of it (more on that later in the book).

Basic Allowance for Subsistence (BAS) – Covering Food Costs

BAS is an additional allowance for food, covering daily meals for service members. As of 2024:

- Enlisted members receive $460 per month
- Officers receive $320 per month

BAS helps offset food costs, but many service members still spend way more than they should on eating out, fast food, and convenience meals.

Bonuses & Special Pay – Extra Opportunities

Beyond base pay and allowances, service members can increase their earnings through bonuses and special pay. Some examples include:

Enlistment & Reenlistment Bonuses – Some MOS (Military Occupational Specialties) offer **$20,000+ bonuses** just for signing or staying in

Hazardous Duty Pay – Extra compensation for dangerous jobs (parachuting, diving, demolitions)

Deployment Pay – Additional pay while stationed in a combat zone

Sea Pay & Flight Pay – Extra earnings for those working in specialized roles

These bonuses add up fast, but many service members blow through them instead of using them wisely.

COMMON FINANCIAL PITFALLS IN THE MILITARY

Even with steady pay, tax-free benefits, and bonuses, many service members still end up struggling financially and it's not because they aren't getting paid enough. It's because bad money habits can erase any financial advantage the military provides. Here are some of the biggest money traps that service members fall into.

1. Over-Reliance on Credit

Credit cards are the military's version of an IED: silent, dangerous, and ready to explode if you're not careful. Walk into any bank near a military base, and you'll immediately be offered a high-limit credit card with "great perks," zero interest for a year, and "exclusive military benefits." Sounds great, right? Wrong. Here's the problem:

Many use credit to fund a lifestyle they can't afford. (*Oh, I can totally pay this off next month!*)

High interest rates (often 20% or more) trap service members in never-ending debt cycles. (*Wait, why is my minimum payment barely touching the balance?*)

Late payments tank credit scores, making it harder to buy a home later on. (*But I NEED that VA Home Loan to work!*)

I've seen E-2s and E-3s rack up over $10,000 in credit card debt before even hitting E-4. Why? Because no one teaches us how credit actually works. We don't think about interest rates, debt-to-income ratios, or the fact that paying only the minimum balance means you'll still be paying off your 55-inch TV in 2037. And before you know it, your entire paycheck is going toward debt payments instead of building wealth.

2. Expensive Car Loans – The Military's Rite of Passage

Every military base has at least three things within a five-mile radius: a strip club, a tattoo shop, and predatory car dealerships. And those dealerships are waiting like hyenas for the next freshly paid service member to walk onto the lot, wide-eyed and ready to sign whatever gets them into that shiny new sports car. How do they trap service members?

- **They approve loans with insanely high interest rates (often 18-25% APR).**
- **They overprice vehicles, knowing service members will pay sticker price without negotiating.**
- **They convince new recruits to buy luxury cars they can't afford.**

I've personally seen E-3s making $2,800 a month get stuck paying $800+ per month for a car payment. That's almost one-third of their paycheck, just for a depreciating asset.

And if that wasn't bad enough, let's add in the fact that insurance for a 22-year-old with a brand-new Mustang is through the roof. Suddenly, half their paycheck is gone before they even get to the barracks. Let me tell you something, when I was young, I got suckered into the car game too. I thought I was making a smart financial decision, only to realize that high-interest car loans are financial quicksand. The best part? That "sweet ride" gets repossessed the moment they miss a payment—because, let's be honest, most E-3s don't have an emergency fund.

3. Lifestyle Inflation – The Silent Killer of Financial Growth

Lifestyle inflation is one of the biggest killers of financial success, and service members fall for it **ALL THE TIME.**

Here's how it works:

You get a promotion → You lease a more expensive car. (*I earned this upgrade!*)

You get a bonus → You take a luxury vacation. (*Margaritas in Cancun, baby!*)

You get BAH → You upgrade to a bigger, more expensive rental. (*That ocean view is totally worth the extra $600 per month!*)

Instead of saving or investing, service members spend every new dollar they make. I see it every single day. Someone makes E-5 or E-6, gets a nice pay bump, and immediately starts spending more. Nicer apartment. Fancy dinners. New gadgets. They justify it with, *"I work hard, I deserve nice things!"* And don't get me wrong, I'm all for enjoying life. But here's the problem: when you spend everything you earn, you'll never build long-term wealth.

I'll never forget my own wake-up call. When I made Chief Petty Officer, I thought, *"Damn, I made it!"* So, what did I do?

Upgraded my lifestyle

Spent money like I was invincible

Kept telling myself I'd "start saving later"

Spoiler alert: later never came. I looked at my bank account one day and realized I was still living paycheck to paycheck, despite making more money than ever. That's when it hit me: the problem wasn't how much I was making, it was how I was spending.

IT'S NOT WHAT YOU MAKE, IT'S WHAT YOU KEEP

The military provides an incredible opportunity to build wealth, but most service members miss the chance because of bad money habits. If you can avoid these three financial traps:

1. **Stop relying on credit for things you don't need**
2. **Don't fall for high-interest car loans that destroy your paycheck**
3. **Resist lifestyle inflation—live below your means and invest the difference**

Then you can set yourself up for financial success while still serving. And trust me, I wish someone had told me all of this when I was an E-3 getting my first "real" paycheck. It would have saved me from years of bad financial decisions. But now that you know, you have the chance to do things differently. Your future wealthy self will thank you.

THE "LACK OF RESOURCES" MYTH – THE BIGGEST EXCUSE IN THE MILITARY

One of the biggest excuses I hear from service members struggling financially is: *"I just don't make enough money to save or invest."* This couldn't be further from the truth. Look, I get it. Military paychecks aren't glamorous, and no one joins the military expecting to get rich. But let's be real—most service members aren't struggling because they're underpaid. They're struggling because they don't manage their money properly.

As Tony Robbins famously said: *"It's not the lack of resources, it's the lack of resourcefulness."* Translation? Most of us have the money, we just waste it. Let me prove it:

- **If you're an E-4 living off base with BAH, you could easily save $500+ per month**
- **If you invested just $200 per month into a Roth IRA starting at 20, you'd have over $500,000 by retirement**
- **If you used your VA Home Loan instead of renting, you'd be building equity instead of throwing money away on rent**

Yet, instead of saving or investing, what do most service members do?

- **Finance a brand-new Mustang at 23% interest**
- **Drop half their paycheck at the strip club the night after payday**
- **DoorDash every meal like they're allergic to grocery stores**

I say this from experience. Back in my early Navy days, I thought I was broke. But in reality? I was just terrible with money. I'd blow half my paycheck within the first seventy-two hours of getting paid; partying, eating out, and buying crap I didn't need. Then I'd spend the next two weeks living off ramen and praying my car wouldn't break down. The worst part? I genuinely believed I was broke. But looking back, if I had just cut back on the dumb spending and put away even $100 per paycheck, I'd be in a much better financial position today.

THE REALITY CHECK: WHERE YOUR MONEY REALLY GOES

Service members aren't broke. But we make dumb financial choices that keep us feeling broke. Let's do some quick math:

Starbucks habit: $6/day = **$180/month**

DoorDash addiction: $25 per meal, 3x a week = **$300+/month**

Weekend bar tab: $50/night, 4 weekends = **$200+/month**

New car payment (with high interest): $800/month

That's almost $1,500 per month that could be invested, saved, or used for something actually important, but instead, it's getting lit on fire. And trust me, I've been there. I remember looking at my bank account one day and thinking: *"Where the hell did all my money go?"* Then I checked my statement and realized I had spent $300 at Chili's in one month. At Chili's. If I had taken even half of what I was blowing on bottomless chips and margaritas and invested it, I'd be sitting on a serious stack of cash today.

HOW TO ACTUALLY BUILD WEALTH WITH WHAT YOU HAVE

The good news? You don't need to make six figures to start building wealth. Instead of saying, *"I don't have enough money to save,"* try saying, *"I need to find better ways to manage what I already have."*

- **Cut out unnecessary spending** (yes, you can survive without daily Starbucks)
- **Live below your means** (do you really need that brand-new truck, or will a used car do the job?)
- **Use your BAH wisely** (house-hack, buy instead of rent, or pocket the difference)
- **Invest early and often** (a little now turns into a lot later)

I wish someone had smacked me upside the head when I was younger and told me this: You will NEVER out-earn bad spending habits. If you can't manage $3,000 a month, you won't magically be better at managing $10,000 a month later on. And if you keep waiting to be rich enough to start saving, guess what? You'll never start.

NO MORE EXCUSES

The problem isn't a lack of money, it's a lack of education, planning, and smart decision-making.

You **CAN** save.

You **CAN** invest.

You **CAN** build wealth—**even on a military paycheck.**

The only question is: are you willing to make the necessary changes to do it? If I could go back and tell 20-year-old me one thing, it would be this: *"Stop wasting money on dumb shit, start investing now, and you'll thank yourself later."* Now that YOU know better, what are you going to do about it?

THE FIRST STEP TO WINNING FINANCIALLY

If you're reading this, you're already ahead of most service members, because you're taking the time to learn. The first step to financial success in the military is understanding your income, avoiding common traps, and shifting your mindset from spending to investing.

I hear and forget. What I write I understand.

TWO
THE REALITY OF MILITARY FINANCES – THE MINDSET SHIFT

THE FOUNDATION OF FINANCIAL LITERACY: YOUR MINDSET COMES FIRST

AS I MENTIONED EARLIER, the military doesn't teach wealth—but let's go deeper into why that mindset sticks. Sure, we get steady paychecks, housing allowances, and benefits that civilians would kill for, but how many service members do you know who are actually wealthy? Exactly. That's because financial success doesn't start with how much money you make, it starts with how you think about money. If you have a broke mindset, you'll stay broke, no matter how big your paycheck is.

When I was growing up, money wasn't something we talked about, unless it was stressing over not having enough of it. I didn't know about investing, saving, or wealth-building. I knew how to float checks (yes, I'm that old). If you don't know what floating a check is, consider yourself lucky; it was a strategy where you'd write a check days before payday, praying that it wouldn't clear before your deposit hit. That, my friends, is the original form of living paycheck to paycheck. And if you don't think that mentality sticks with you, think again.

When I was young, I thought "being good with money" meant paying my bills on time and not bouncing a check (which was a serious accomplishment, by the way). The idea of building wealth? That was for rich people. I was just trying to make it to payday without running out of gas. But here's what I learned the hard way: the way you were raised to think about money is NOT the way you need to think about money moving forward.

The Lesson That Changed Everything: Rich Dad vs. Poor Dad

One of the biggest lessons I learned was from *Rich Dad, Poor Dad* by Robert Kiyosaki, a book that completely changed the way I think about money. Seriously, before I read this book, I thought financial success just meant getting a good job, working hard, and slowly climbing the ladder. I had no idea that I was following a script designed to keep me trapped in the cycle of paycheck-to-paycheck living.

Kiyosaki explained that most people are conditioned to work for money, but the wealthy? They make money work for them. At first, I thought this was some motivational mumbo jumbo. I mean, *"Yeah, sure, rich people don't have to work. Must be nice."* But the more I read, the more I realized, this was exactly why so many people struggle financially. For most of us, we were taught the **Poor Dad mentality** growing up:

- **Get a stable job**
- **Earn a steady paycheck**
- **Pay your bills and debt first**
- **Save whatever's left over (which is usually nothing)**

This was my exact mindset for years. When I joined the Navy, I thought, *"I have a guaranteed paycheck, benefits, and job security; what else do I need?"* Then, reality hit.

I watched senior enlisted personnel who had served twenty plus years retire broke, scrambling to find a civilian job to make ends meet. I saw

Sailors drowning in credit card debt and driving $50,000 Mustangs while living in the barracks. I experienced firsthand what it was like to rack up tens of thousands of dollars in credit card debt with no plan to get out of it. That's when I started realizing that the entire system is designed to keep you just comfortable enough to survive, but never truly free.

THE *RICH DAD* WAKE-UP CALL

What Kiyosaki taught in *Rich Dad, Poor Dad* was that this traditional way of handling money was (and still is) a trap. The **Rich Dad mentality** is completely different:

- **Buy assets that make you money**
- **Use your money to create passive income**
- **Pay yourself first, before paying bills**
- **Think like an investor, not a worker**

This book completely shattered my belief system about money. Up until that point, I thought the goal was to make more money. But Kiyosaki made me realize:

It's not how much money you make—it's what you do with it.

There are millionaires who went bankrupt and people making $50,000 a year who retire financially free because of how they handle money. I was living in the **Poor Dad mindset:** thinking that working harder, getting promoted, and earning a bigger paycheck would eventually lead to financial freedom. But this book made me realize:

If your money isn't working for you, you'll ALWAYS have to work for money.

HOW THIS CHANGED MY LIFE

When I first read this book, I had zero assets, a mountain of debt, and no real plan for financial independence. I started small:

- Instead of **blowing every extra dollar I made**, I started **investing**
- Instead of thinking of my paycheck as the end goal, I started **figuring out how to turn my money into more money**
- Instead of following the "**save whatever's left**" mentality, I started **paying myself first**, treating investments like a bill that had to be paid every month

I also realized that **real estate was one of the most powerful wealth-building tools available, especially for military members.**

If I had kept following the Poor Dad mentality, I'd still be struggling, working extra jobs just to keep my head above water.

Instead, I started thinking like an investor:

I bought real estate instead of renting

I started learning about **passive income streams** (instead of just working more hours)

I made **my money work for me, so I didn't have to work forever**

And guess what? This works for ANYONE. You don't have to be rich to start thinking like the rich. You just have to stop thinking like the poor. The reality is, no one is coming to save you financially.

Not the military

Not your boss

Not the government

It's up to YOU to learn the rules of money and start playing to win.

So, are you going to keep following the **Poor Dad mindset**, or are you ready to start thinking like **Rich Dad?**

THE MILITARY'S RELATIONSHIP WITH MONEY: JUST ENOUGH TO GET BY

The military is fantastic at paying you just enough to survive, but not enough to thrive. It's like they dangle a financial carrot just out of reach to keep you moving forward. They give you enough money to stay afloat, but if you don't know how to manage it, you'll spend twenty plus years in uniform and still retire broke.

Let me break it down for you.

THE MILITARY'S PAY BREAKDOWN (AND HOW WE WASTE IT)

Base Pay – Your steady paycheck, the foundation of your income. You get promoted, you make more—but somehow, that extra money magically disappears. Every time you get a raise, you suddenly need a new car, a bigger apartment, or a fancy watch to match your new rank. (*Looking at you, Staff Sergeant with the Rolex.*)

BAH– This is where the military literally hands you money for housing. And yet, too many service members waste it on expensive rentals instead of using it to buy a home and build equity. I've seen guys blow 100% of their BAH on luxury apartments because they wanted a rooftop pool and a "sick view," instead of house hacking and letting tenants pay their mortgage for them. (*News flash: The view doesn't build wealth.*)

BAS – Aka your "food money." And if you're anything like I was as a young Sailor, BAS usually meant blowing it on takeout, energy drinks, and beer. The DFAC (Dining Facility) food was free, but did I eat there? Nope. I was too busy DoorDashing Panda Express five times a week. Then payday came, and I was mystified as to why I was broke.

Special Pay & Bonuses – Extra money for deployments, hazardous duty, or specialized jobs. This sounds like free money, right? Until you blow it on a brand-new F-150 with a 25% interest rate or a Harley you "needed" after watching Sons of Anarchy. (*I'm not saying I did this... but I definitely thought about it.*)

THE REAL PROBLEM: LIFESTYLE INFLATION

The problem isn't that the military doesn't pay well, it's that most service members spend every damn dollar they make.

You get a pay raise → You upgrade your lifestyle

You get BAH → You rent the nicest place you can afford

You get a bonus → You finance a new car

The truth is, if you don't control lifestyle inflation, you will always be broke, no matter how much money you make. And here's the crazy part...E-1s are broke, but so are O-6s. The only difference? O-6s just have fancier debt. I've met junior enlisted who are financially free before hitting E-6 and officers who are drowning in debt despite making six figures. Why? Because it's not about how much you make, it's about how you manage what you make.

THE MILITARY DOESN'T TEACH YOU THIS... BUT I WILL

Think about it: you train for combat, you prepare for deployments, you memorize SOPs and regulations, but did anyone ever sit you down and teach you how to build wealth?

Nope. In fact, the system kind of counts on you being financially clueless.

They want you comfortable enough to keep re-enlisting.

They don't want you financially independent before you hit 20 years.

They want you needing that next promotion just to make ends meet.

That's why this book exists.

The military won't teach you how to use your money to buy assets, invest, or escape the paycheck-to-paycheck trap, but I will. Because here's the truth: financial freedom isn't about making more money, it's about learning how to keep and grow the money you already make. So, the question is: are you going to keep playing the game, or are you ready to start winning it?

THE CONSUMER TRAP: HOW SOCIETY KEEPS YOU BROKE

If you've ever been stationed near a military base, you've seen the predatory businesses just waiting to take your money:

- **Car dealerships** offering *"military financing"* (aka 25% interest loans on a Mustang you can't afford)
- **Furniture stores** promising *"No payments for 12 months!"* (and then slamming you with an insane interest rate if you don't pay in full)
- **Payday lenders** charging *ridiculous fees just to give you an advance on your own damn money*

And the worst part? We fall for it. Why? Because we're raised in a debt-based society that teaches us to borrow money instead of building wealth.

- *You NEED credit to buy things.*
- *You NEED a car loan to get a reliable car.*
- *You NEED to finance furniture because who the hell can afford a $3,000 couch upfront?*

Spoiler alert: You don't ***NEED*** any of that.

THE MILITARY'S ROLE IN THE CONSUMER TRAP

We're trained from birth to be consumers, and the military is no different.

- You get a raise? You upgrade your lifestyle.
- You get a bonus? You spend it before it even hits your account.
- You get BAH? You immediately find the most expensive apartment you can afford.

It's a trap. And the craziest part? It doesn't matter how much you make. I've seen junior enlisted and officers alike fall into the same financial sinkhole. I've known O-4s who are drowning in debt, and I've met E-4s who are financially set for life. It's not about how much money you make, it's about how you use it. And if you're not careful, the system will keep you broke until the day you retire.

THE BACKSTORY OF MY $40,000 WAKE-UP CALL

When I first became an adult, I did what most young service members do: I treated credit cards like free money. It started innocently enough…one day, I was maxing out a card at Best Buy (*because obviously, an E-3 needs a surround sound system and a giant TV*). The next day, I was signing up for another credit card because they offered a *0% balance transfer for 12 months.*

So, I transferred my debt to the new card. Then I maxed out the old card again. And the cycle continued. At the time, it didn't seem like a big deal. Everyone had debt, right? Then, reality hit me like a freight train. By the time my wife moved to the U.S. from Sweden, I was so deep in credit card debt that my salary that couldn't even cover the interest payments. Welcome to marriage, honey!

I remember sitting down with my credit card statements, realizing that even though I was making payments every month, my balance wasn't going down. I was paying the minimum balance, thinking I was being responsible, until I realized that at this rate, I'd be paying off that debt until the next century. That was the moment I had my financial wake-up call. I had two choices:

1. Keep doing what I was doing and stay broke forever

2. Change my mindset and take control of my money

THE MOMENT I STOPPED PLAYING THE GAME

That was the turning point. I realized that credit card companies, car dealerships, payday lenders weren't here to help me. They were here to trap me. And I fell for it. But not anymore. I made one final transfer; this time, to a consolidation loan. I cut up my credit cards (*well, most of them*), and I swore to never be in that kind of debt again. And you know what? I never was.

THE LESSON? DON'T PLAY THEIR GAME—BEAT IT

I share this story because I know I'm not the only one who's been there. I've seen too many service members fall into the same trap, financing a lifestyle they can't afford, thinking they're *"building credit,"* when really, they're just digging a hole.

The good news? You don't have to play the game.

- **You don't have to finance a new car**
- **You don't have to rack up credit card debt**
- **You don't have to be another statistic**

Instead, you can learn from my mistakes, take control of your money, and build real wealth. The choice is yours.

THE FIRST STEP: PAY YOURSELF FIRST

If you take **nothing else** from this chapter, take this: **PAY YOURSELF FIRST.**

This was the biggest lesson I learned from *Rich Dad, Poor Dad,* what I call the Purple Bible of financial freedom. But I'll be honest, I didn't fully understand it at first. Most people, including me, have done the exact opposite for a long time.

- **Get paid**
- **Pay all the bills**
- **Spend what's left**
- **Save and invest? Maybe next month**

And that's how you stay broke forever. But the wealthy? They pay themselves first. They take their money, invest it, and then use what's left to cover expenses.

WHY THIS SHIFT IS A GAME-CHANGER

Back in the day, when I was a young Sailor, I did what every other young service member did, I got paid and immediately spent it. Bills, food, going out, maybe paying off a little bit of debt (*but not really*), and whatever was left over? Well, that was my *"fun money."* And guess what? There was never anything left over. I was always in that same cycle, constantly feeling like I was just scraping by, even when I got a raise.

It wasn't until I made one simple shift that everything changed: I treated my investments like a bill. I told myself, *"If I can commit to paying my phone bill, I can commit to paying my future self."* And you know what? It worked.

HOW TO PAY YOURSELF FIRST

It's simple, but it takes discipline:

1. **Every paycheck, set aside a percentage of your income for savings or investments FIRST**
2. **THEN pay your bills**
3. **THEN spend what's left**

Instead of committing to a fixed dollar amount, commit to a percentage of your income; start with 5% or 10%. Why? Because as your income grows, so will your savings and investments. If you start by saving 10% of your paycheck, then every time you get a raise, your investments automatically increase without any extra effort on your part. If you get used to living on 90% of your income now, it won't feel like a sacrifice later.

THE MILITARY MINDSET & PAYING YOURSELF FIRST

Now, I get it; when you're in the military, you're not exactly rolling in cash (*unless you're a flag officer, in which case, good for you*). But here's where it gets interesting; you already know how to budget; you just don't realize it. Think about it:

- You know how to prioritize your gear, your uniform, your training before everything else
- You know how to follow SOPs (Standard Operating Procedures) and stick to a plan
- You know how to execute a mission with precision

So why not apply that same discipline to your finances?

The "No Money to Save" Excuse

I've heard it all before: *"Travis, I don't have enough money to save! I can barely cover my bills!"* Oh really?

Let's break it down.

You don't have enough to save, but you somehow have money for:

That $7 Starbucks coffee.

That new PS5 game.

That Uber Eats delivery (*when you literally live on base with a chow hall*).

That bar tab on a Friday night.

I say this with love: **STOP LYING TO YOURSELF.**

When I was a young Sailor making barely enough to survive, I still managed to find money for dumb stuff. One day, I had to have a hard conversation with myself. I looked at my bank statement (*which I avoided for months because, let's be honest, checking your balance was sometimes an extreme sport*) and I saw how much money I was wasting.

Hundreds on fast food

More on subscriptions I didn't even remember signing up for

And don't even get me started on how much I spent at Best Buy

And yet, I was **convinced** I had "no money to save." Sound familiar?

THE MILITARY HACK TO PAYING YOURSELF FIRST

Here's how I forced myself to start saving:

Step 1: Make it Automatic – I set up an **automatic transfer** so that the second my paycheck hit, a percentage went straight into an investment account before I even saw it. *(Out of sight, out of mind.)*

Step 2: Start Small – I started with just 5% of my paycheck, and after a few months, I barely noticed the money missing.

Step 3: Increase Over Time – Every time I got a raise, promotion, or bonus, I increased my percentage before I had a chance to spend it.

The Results?

After a few months, I barely noticed the money missing from my paycheck—but my investment account was growing. After a few years, that habit turned into real wealth. After a decade, I had multiple investment accounts, real estate properties, and financial freedom.

And you can do the same.

The Bottom Line

Look, you don't need to be a Wall Street genius to build wealth. You just need one habit: **PAY YOURSELF FIRST.**

- If you can commit to paying your bills,
- If you can commit to waking up at 0600 for PT,
- If you can commit to serving your country,

Then you can commit to paying yourself first. Start with just 5% and work your way up. And trust me: your future self will thank you.

No More Excuses – Start Now

People love to make excuses for why they can't start:

- *"I don't make enough money."*
- *"I'll start when I pay off my car."*
- *"It's too late, I should have started years ago."*

Bullshit. Excuses are like assholes: everyone's got one. The truth is, you don't need a high income to start winning financially. You just need to use what you have smarter.

- You have guaranteed income
- You have benefits civilians don't get
- You have a support system to help you succeed

You just have to take that first step.

UNDERSTANDING ASSETS VS. LIABILITIES: THE GAME-CHANGER FOR MILITARY WEALTH

Let's pause for a second and talk about two words that can either make or break your financial future: **assets** and **liabilities**. I know, it sounds like accounting jargon, but if you don't understand the difference between these two, you will stay broke. I didn't grasp this early on, and it cost me years of progress and tens of thousands of dollars.

So, what's the difference?

An asset is something that **puts money in your pocket**.

A liability is something that **takes money out of your pocket**.

Let's simplify it even more:

Item

Asset or Liability?

Why?

Rental property

Asset

It produces monthly rental income and appreciates over time.

Your personal residence

Liability (usually)

Unless it's generating income (e.g. house hacking), it costs you money each month.

Credit card debt

Liability

You're paying interest; money is leaving your pocket.

Stocks or index funds

Asset

They generate dividends and grow in value.

A financed car

Liability

You make payments every month, and it depreciates in value.

A business that cash flows

Asset

It earns income for you, even while you sleep.

This is the *Rich Dad vs. Poor Dad* mindset in action. Poor Dad says, "Buy a nice house, a new car, and some nice clothes because you earned it." Rich Dad says, "Use your money to buy assets first, then let those assets pay for the lifestyle."

THE MILITARY TRAP: CONFUSING COMFORT WITH WEALTH

Too many of us in uniform fall for the trap of **thinking liabilities are assets**. You get your re-enlistment bonus and blow it on a new truck, telling yourself, "It's worth it, it's mine!" But let's be real: if it's not paying you monthly, it's not an asset. It's draining you.

- That car payment? Liability.
- That "free" furniture with 0% APR? Liability.
- That second PS5 for your barracks room? Definitely a liability.

The military sets us up for this. They give us **guaranteed income**, **housing**, and **food allowances**, and we mistake that comfort for financial stability. So we start stacking liabilities, one after another, until we're drowning in monthly payments with nothing to show for it but depreciating toys and mounting stress.

Why Assets Matter More Than Income

I know Sailors who make $60K a year and are on the path to financial independence because they own assets. I also know officers making $120K who are dead broke, buried in car notes and credit card debt. **It's not your income—it's what your income buys.**

If your paycheck disappears every month on things that don't make money, you're building someone else's wealth, not your own.

"The rich buy assets. The poor only have expenses. The middle class buys liabilities they think are assets." ~ Robert Kiyosaki

That quote slapped me in the face when I first read it. Because I was the guy who thought buying a big house or a new car meant I was "winning." But I wasn't. I was just sinking deeper into the liability trap.

THE SERVICE MEMBER ADVANTAGE

Here's the crazy part: we in the military have an **unfair advantage,** we just don't use it right. Our steady income, housing allowance, and benefits create the perfect opportunity to start acquiring **real assets**:

- Use BAH to buy a **multi-family home** and live in one unit while renting out the others.
- Take your deployment savings and invest in **low-cost index funds**.
- Partner with a veteran buddy and invest in a **cash-flowing real estate deal**.
- Use SkillBridge or VA Education Benefits to learn skills that create **income-generating side businesses**.

The point is this: once I understood that **assets buy freedom** and **liabilities steal it**, I started making decisions like an investor. I stopped asking, "Can I afford this?" and started asking, "Will this make me money?"

This mental shift, from consumer to investor, is the most powerful change a service member can make. It's the foundation of everything we'll cover in the rest of this book. Because if you don't understand the difference between what grows your wealth and what drains it, you'll never break free from the paycheck-to-paycheck cycle.

So ask yourself:

- What am I spending my money on?
- Is it building wealth or just buying comfort?
- Am I stacking assets or just stacking payments?

When I was on active duty, I thought I was doing everything right. I showed up on time, performed with excellence, and took pride in my uniform. But I was still broke. It wasn't until I stopped chasing shiny things and started chasing cash flow that things changed. I looked around and saw fellow service members financing cars they couldn't afford, blowing bonuses on vacations, and living paycheck to paycheck despite steady income. It wasn't a lack of money; it was a lack of mindset.

Thinking like an investor means asking: how can I make every dollar work for me? Can my paycheck buy time, freedom, or long-term growth? You begin to realize that financial independence isn't about how much you earn—it's about how much you keep and what that money does when you're not looking. The rich don't work for money. They make money work for them.

That's the shift. It's not about deprivation, it's about direction. No one joins the military to just get by. We train, fight, and lead with purpose. Why should our finances be any different? It's time to train for financial war, fight for financial freedom, and lead our families to generational wealth.

Don't just survive your time in service. Use it. Build with it. And leave with more than stories; leave with assets that continue to serve you long after your service ends.

Your mission, starting now, is to think like the rich—because financial freedom starts with buying assets.

FINAL THOUGHT: YOUR FINANCIAL FREEDOM STARTS WITH YOUR MINDSET

If you don't change your mindset, you'll never change your financial situation. Here's what you need to do today:

Stop thinking like a consumer

Start paying yourself first

Stop making excuses and understand the difference between an asset and a liability

Take action NOW

In Chapter 3, we'll break down how to build a bulletproof budget, one that actually works for military life and puts you on the path to financial success. But first, take a moment to commit to this:

Pay yourself first.

Live below your means.

Invest in your future.

Do this, and I promise you—your financial future will change forever.

I hear and forget. What I write I understand.

THREE
THE FOUR STEPS TO BUDGETING – YOUR MISSION PLAN FOR FINANCIAL SUCCESS

"A BUDGET IS TELLING YOUR MONEY WHERE TO GO INSTEAD OF WONDERING WHERE IT WENT."

~Dave Ramsey

THE BATTLE PLAN **for Your Money**

In the military, everything runs on a mission plan.

- **Deployments?** Planned to the smallest detail.
- **Training exercises?** Coordinated with strategy and risk assessments.
- **Maintenance schedules?** Locked down tighter than your chief's locked desk drawer.

No one just wakes up and says, *"Hey, let's deploy today and see what happens!"* So why do so many service members approach their finances with zero planning? I can't tell you how many Sailors I've seen completely clueless about where their paycheck actually goes. They check their bank balance and wonder, *"Wait...where did all my money go?"*

Well, a budget is how you find out.

You Can't Win a War Without a Strategy

Here's the truth: if you don't control your money, your money will control you. When I was younger, I thought I was financially responsible because I paid my bills on time (most of the time). But in reality, I was just winging it. My financial strategy consisted of:

1. **Checking my bank balance daily and hoping I still had money**
2. **Paying whatever bill was screaming the loudest**
3. **Spending whatever was left**
4. **Wondering why I was broke by mid-month**

Sound familiar? I wasn't *planning* my finances; I was just reacting to them. The result?

- **Constant financial stress**
- **No savings**
- **Way too much debt**

And yet, I still somehow had money for weekend bar tabs, electronics I didn't need, and impulse purchases that made zero sense. It wasn't until I took control of my money and created a real budget that everything changed.

BUDGETING = FINANCIAL FREEDOM (NOT FINANCIAL PRISON)

Let's clear something up right now: **Budgeting is NOT about restriction.** It's not about:

- Cutting out all the fun
- Never spending money on things you enjoy
- Eating ramen noodles forever

Budgeting is about control. It's about giving yourself:

The ability to **spend without guilt** because you planned for it

The power to **save and invest** for the future

The freedom to **live comfortably** without constantly stressing about money

Think of a budget like a deployment mission plan. You know where your money is going before it even leaves your account. Instead of wondering, *"Where did all my money go?"* you'll be saying, *"Hell yeah, I know exactly where my money is, and it's working for me."*

WHY MOST PEOPLE DON'T BUDGET (AND WHY THAT'S BS)

Let's address the top excuses people make for not budgeting:

"I don't have time." Oh, but you have time to scroll Instagram for hours? A budget takes less than thirty minutes a month.

"I don't make enough money to budget." A budget isn't just for rich people. It's the **ONLY** way to stop living paycheck to paycheck and actually build wealth.

"Budgeting is too complicated." Nope. You don't need fancy spreadsheets or finance degrees. If you can make a basic mission plan, you can make a budget.

"I like to be spontaneous with my money." Translation: *"I like being broke and stressed all the time."*

"I don't need a budget, I'm doing fine." Really? How much did you save last month? If you don't know, you need a budget.

The Military-Grade Budgeting Plan

This chapter will break down a four-step approach to budgeting that actually works.

This isn't some finance guru nonsense about cutting out lattes and living like a monk.

This is real budgeting for real military families—a plan that:

Gives you financial control

Lets you enjoy your money responsibly

Sets you up for long-term success

Because at the end of the day, you worked hard for your money, now it's time to make it work for you.

STEP 1: COMMIT TO A MONTHLY BUDGET - KNOW WHERE YOUR MONEY IS GOING

When you're in the military, every mission has a plan. You don't just roll out of bed and stumble into an operation hoping everything works out. You have strategy, logistics, and contingencies in place. So why would you treat your money any differently?

Committing to a monthly budget is the first step in taking control of your financial future.

Now, I know what you're thinking: *"Budgeting is boring, time-consuming, and makes life less fun."* I used to think the same thing, until I found myself broke, drowning in debt, and wondering why I was working so hard but never getting ahead. That's when I realized that a budget isn't about restriction, it's about freedom. It allows you to tell your money where to go instead of wondering where it went. There are two budgets you should create:

1. **Your Current Budget** – Write down everything you're actually spending money on. No sugarcoating. If you're dropping $300 a month on DoorDash, own it. If your car payment is eating up half your paycheck, write it down. If you lie to yourself on this step, you're only hurting your future.
2. **Your Survivability Budget** – This is your **bare minimum survival** number. It includes:
   - Housing (Rent/Mortgage)
   - Utilities (Electricity, Water, Internet)
   - Transportation (Gas, Insurance, Car Payment)
   - Food (Groceries—not Chick-fil-A drive-thru runs)
   - Healthcare

This does NOT include:

- Your Netflix subscription
- New Jordans
- DoorDash, UberEats, or that $8 Starbucks habit
- That PS5 you just *had* to have

Once you compare these two budgets, you'll see the delta (difference) between them. That's where you can start trimming the fat and putting money toward your future.

The $200 Challenge

Now, I'm not going to tell you to go full monk mode and never enjoy life, but I want you to make one small sacrifice each month. Take just one night of going out, one unnecessary expense, one impulse buy, and instead, set aside $200. This isn't just some random number. That $200 is about to change your life. Stick with me, and I'll show you how.

STEP 2: BUILD AN EMERGENCY FUND – YOUR FINANCIAL BODY ARMOR

In the military, you never go into battle without your gear. Your emergency fund is your financial body armor. Here's a scary stat: the average American has less than $500 in savings. That means one unexpected car repair, medical bill, or emergency could send them spiraling into debt. And once you start swiping the credit card for emergencies, it's game over. So, what's the solution?

How Much Should You Save?

Your emergency fund should include **at least three months of your survivability budget** (not your full lifestyle budget, just what you need to survive). If you want to be extra safe, **six months is ideal.**

Where to Keep Your Emergency Fund

High-Yield Savings Account (Ally, Capital One 360, etc.) – This keeps your money separate from your daily checking account and earns some interest.

Not in Stocks or Investments – Your emergency fund is not an investment, it's a safety net. Keep it liquid and accessible.

Warning: Don't hoard too much cash. Savings accounts earn less than 1% interest, while inflation eats away at your money at 3-9% per year. Three to six months is enough, any extra should be working for you elsewhere.

STEP 3: GET OUT OF DEBT – ELIMINATE FINANCIAL HANDCUFFS

We live in a debt-based society, and trust me, the system is designed to keep you in debt. Credit card companies, payday lenders, car dealerships—they all make a fortune off service members. They offer "special military financing" that sounds helpful, but in reality, they're just setting you up for a lifetime of payments. But not you. You're about to break free from the debt trap and start making your money work for YOU instead of handing it over to the banks every month.

Good Debt vs. Bad Debt

Not all debt is bad. Some debt can actually help you build wealth, while other types will keep you broke forever.

Good Debt (Wealth-Building Debt)

- **Mortgage** (buying property that appreciates over time)
- **Reasonable Student Loans** (only if it increases earning potential)
- **Car Loan** (if necessary for work, but NOT for a luxury car you can't afford)

Bad Debt (Wealth-Destroying debt)

- **Credit Cards** (high-interest rates that trap you in never-ending payments)
- **Payday Loans** (the fastest way to go broke)
- **High-Interest Personal Loans** (anything above 10% APR is robbing you blind)

HOW TO GET OUT OF DEBT – THE SNOWBALL EFFECT

Remember that $200 I asked you to set aside? Here's how we use it to obliterate your bad debt:

1. **List all of your debts from smallest to largest balance.**
2. **Make the minimum payments on all but the smallest debt.**
3. **Take that $200 and add it to the payment for your smallest debt.**
4. **Once that debt is gone, roll that full payment into your next highest debt.**
5. **Repeat until you're completely debt-free.**

Example:

- You have a $500 store credit card with a $100 minimum payment
- Instead of paying just $100, you add the $200 you saved, making the total $300 per month
- In two months, that debt is gone
- Now take that $300 and roll it into your next highest debt
- Keep rolling payments forward until you wipe out all bad debt

This snowball effect speeds up debt repayment and gets you out of bad debt faster than you ever thought possible.

Why Minimum Payments Will Keep You in Debt FOREVER

Here's what credit card companies don't want you to know: If you only pay the minimum payment on a credit card, **you will never pay it off.** That's because the minimum payment is designed to only cover the interest, **NOT** the principal (the actual amount you owe).

Let's break it down:

- You have a $5,000 balance on a credit card with a 20% interest rate
- Your minimum payment is $125 per month
- If you only make minimum payments, it will take you over 30 years to pay it off
- And by the time you do? You will have paid more than $15,000, THREE TIMES the original amount you borrowed!

That's how banks and credit card companies get rich: by keeping you in debt for as long as possible while you barely chip away at the principal. So, if you're only paying the minimum, STOP. Increase your payments as much as you can and use the snowball effect to destroy your balances as fast as possible.

Alternative Strategy – The Consolidation Loan Approach

While the snowball method is great for tackling debt one-by-one, if your total debt is overwhelming, there's another option: **a consolidation loan.** I know this strategy well because it's exactly what I had to do when I was drowning in credit card debt.

How It Works:

A **consolidation loan** allows you to:

Combine **all your high-interest debts into a single, lower-interest loan**

Lock **in a fixed repayment term** (so you have an exact payoff date)

Save **money on interest**, making it easier to get ahead

My Personal Experience – Crawling Back to Mom for Help

I remember the day I finally hit my breaking point. I was deep in debt, barely covering the minimum payments, and realizing I was on a financial treadmill going nowhere. I tried to get a debt consolidation loan on my own, but guess what? My credit was garbage. No lender wanted to touch me. That's when I had to do something I never wanted to do I went back to my mom and asked her to co-sign for me.

Now, let's be clear this was NOT an easy conversation. "Mom, I've got $40,000 in credit card debt, and I need your help." Yeah, that went over really well. But my mom knew I was serious about getting my finances under control, so she co-signed a consolidation loan for me. That single loan:

- Paid off all my credit cards instantly
- Reduced my interest rate from 20-25% down to around 5%
- Gave me one single payment instead of juggling multiple due dates

For the next five years, I stuck to the repayment plan like my financial life depended on it (because it did). And when I made that final payment? It felt like the biggest win of my life. That was the moment I promised myself: never again. I'd never fall into the debt trap like that again, and I'd do everything in my power to help others avoid it too.

Which Debt Strategy Should You Use?

Use the Snowball Effect if you have several smaller debts and want quick wins to keep momentum going.

Use a Consolidation Loan if you have a large amount of debt spread across multiple high-interest accounts and need a structured, long-term repayment plan.

Either way, the goal is the same: eliminate your bad debt and stop letting interest payments rob your future. Once you're out of debt, the next step is the most important shift of all: learning how to pay yourself first and start building wealth.

STEP 4: PAY YOURSELF FIRST - THE KEY TO WEALTH

Do I sound like a broken record? Maybe because this is an incredibly important concept. PAY YOURSELF FIRST! Most people do this:

1. **Pay bills**
2. **Spend money**
3. **Invest whatever is left** (which is usually nothing)

But wealthy people **flip the script:**

1. **Invest first**
2. **Then pay bills**
3. **Then spend what's left**

This is the single most important financial habit you can develop.

How to Pay Yourself First:

1. **Set up automatic deductions** to savings and investments (TSP, Roth IRA, brokerage accounts)
2. **Treat your investments like a bill**: make it a priority, not an afterthought
3. **Start with a percentage, not a dollar amount** – Instead of saying *"I'll invest $200,"* commit to investing **15% of your total income,** that way, as your income grows, your investments grow too

Why This Works

If you pay your bills first and spend next, you'll never have money left over to invest. But if you pay yourself first, you'll automatically adjust your lifestyle to fit whatever is left. Think about it like this: if the government decided to take an extra 10% in taxes tomorrow, you'd complain, but you'd adjust. Treat your future self with the same respect.

TYING IT ALL TOGETHER: THE FOUR STEPS OF BUDGETING

These four steps are designed to build on each other.

1. **Budgeting** helps you find extra money.
2. **An emergency fund** prevents you from using credit cards for unexpected expenses.
3. **Eliminating debt** frees up more money to invest.
4. **Paying yourself first** builds **long-term wealth.**

When you combine all four steps, you unlock true financial freedom.

And remember that $200 challenge? If you saved and invested just $200 per month, in thirty years with compound interest, you'd have over $500,000. That's the power of a budget that actually works.

FINAL THOUGHT: BUDGETING IS YOUR FINANCIAL WEAPON

By following these four steps, you will take control of your money and stop living paycheck to paycheck. Here's your mission:

- **Track your spending for thirty days and categorize every expense as "Essential" or "Optional"**
- **Cut out wasteful expenses**
- **Build your emergency fund**
- **Eliminate debt using the snowball method**
- **Pay yourself first**

I hear and forget. What I write I understand.

FOUR
IMPROVING AND MAINTAINING CREDIT

"GOOD CREDIT IS LIKE MONEY IN THE BANK"

– My Mom Was Right

MY MOM USED to say this phrase all the time when I was growing up: *"Good credit is like money in the bank."* At the time, I didn't fully understand what she meant. But after a few painful financial lessons, I finally realized just how spot on she was.

See, your credit score isn't just a number, it's your financial reputation. It tells banks, lenders, and even landlords how trustworthy you are with money. And just like in the military, your reputation can either open doors or slam them shut in your face. If you have bad credit, lenders see you as a high risk; meaning they assume you're more likely to miss payments, default on loans, or even declare bankruptcy. To protect themselves, they hit you with sky-high interest rates or deny you credit altogether.

But if you have good credit, the game changes completely. You're suddenly the VIP of the financial world; banks trust you; lenders offer you the best deals, and you get access to low-interest rates, higher credit limits, and better loan terms. That's why good credit is like money in the bank, because the better your credit, the more money you save when borrowing.

WHY CREDIT SCORES MATTER MORE THAN YOU THINK

Most people assume credit only matters when getting a loan, but let me tell you, bad credit can haunt you in ways you never expected.

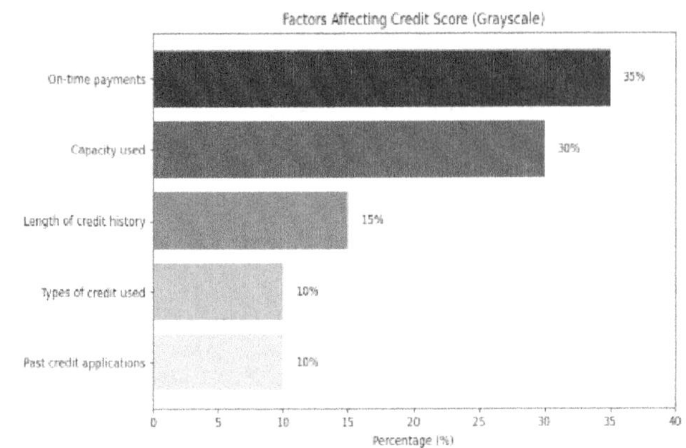

- **Want to buy a home?** Bad credit means **higher mortgage rates**—which can cost you tens of thousands of dollars over the life of the loan
- **Need a car?** Lenders will jack up your interest rate so high that you'll be paying for two cars instead of one
- **Applying for a job?** Many employers check credit reports before hiring, because **they want to see if you're financially responsible**
- **Trying to rent a place?** Landlords run credit **checks, and if your score is bad, they might refuse to rent to you**
- **Getting insurance?** Some companies charge higher premiums for people with low credit scores, even on car insurance

Credit affects almost every major financial decision you'll make, so protecting it should be a top priority.

LEARNING THE HARD WAY: MY $250,000 TENANT NIGHTMARE

Now, I wish I could say I've always had perfect credit, but that would be a massive lie. One of my biggest financial horror stories happened when I rented out a property, thinking I was making a smart financial move. But instead of collecting rent checks and building wealth, I ended up dealing with a tenant from hell. This was a career bad tenant who knew every loophole in the system to scam landlords.

Here's how it went down:

1. They paid **one month's rent upfront**, making everything seem normal.
2. After that? **Not a single payment.**
3. They knew the **tenant protection laws** inside and out, which meant I **couldn't just kick them out.**
4. **Nine months** later, after a **long, expensive eviction process**, I finally regained possession of my home.
5. **By then, the damage was done, literally.** My home had over **$250,000 in damages**, from trashed floors to holes in the walls.

Because of this disaster, I was forced to **short-sell the home**, which **tanked my credit score**. And if that wasn't bad enough? **That bank blacklisted me.** I can never borrow from that institution again. This was one of my biggest financial wake-up calls. Even though I didn't personally miss any payments, my credit took a massive hit because of how the situation unfolded. This is why I preach credit protection like it's a combat mission—because if you don't defend your credit, you can get wiped out before you even see the enemy coming.

THE FOUR KEYS TO GOOD CREDIT: THE SECRET TO WINNING THE CREDIT GAME

If you've made it this far, you already know that good credit = financial power. But how do you actually build and maintain good credit?

Your **credit score is determined by five main factors**:

Payment history – Do you pay on time? (**35% of your score**)

Credit utilization – How much of your available credit are you using? (**30%**)

Length of credit history – How long have your accounts been open? (**15%**)

Types of credit – Do you have a mix of loans and credit cards? (**10%**)

New credit inquiries – Have you opened too many new accounts? (**10%**)

So, what's the game plan for crushing your credit score? Follow these four key principles:

Principle #1: Pay All Bills on Time – No Exceptions

If there's only one rule you follow, make it this one. Payment history makes up 35% of your score, making it the single most important factor in your credit health.

Key Rules to Follow:

Set up automatic payments for all your bills, so you never miss a due date

Even if you can only afford the minimum payment, pay it on time, late payments stay on your credit report for seven years

Missing a payment by just one day can drop your score by fifty plus points

Fun Fact (or maybe not-so-fun): When I was younger and dumber, I ignored a $20 minimum payment on a store credit card because I figured, *"Eh, what's the worst that can happen?"* Spoiler alert: It destroyed my credit score for months, and I ended up paying WAY more in interest and fees. Lesson learned: **NEVER** be late on a payment.

Also, let's tie this back to the golden rule of budgeting: PAY YOURSELF FIRST. That means investing in your future like it's a bill. But when it comes to credit, paying your actual bills on time is non-negotiable.

Principle #2: Keep Credit Balances Low (Credit Utilization Ratio)

Your credit utilization ratio is a fancy way of saying: *"How much of your available credit are you actually using?"*

Why this matters:

- Credit utilization makes up 30% of your credit score
- The higher your balances are, the more it hurts your score, even if you pay on time
- Keep your balance below 30% of your total credit limit

Pro Tips:

- Pay off your balances in full every month if possible
- If you carry a balance, spread it across multiple cards to avoid maxing out any single account
- Increase your credit limit (but don't use it); this automatically lowers your utilization ratio

Example:

Let's say you have a total credit limit of $10,000 across all your cards.

- If you carry a $3,500 balance, you're using 35%—bad for your score
- If you pay it down to $2,500 or less, you're under 25%, which is much better

- If you keep it under 10% ($1,000 or less)—you're winning the credit game

Bonus Tip: If you've had a card for a while and used it responsibly, ask your bank for a credit limit increase, but DON'T use the extra credit! This lowers your utilization ratio and boosts your score.

Principle #3: Keep Your Oldest Credit Accounts Open – Your Credit History is Your Resume

Length of credit history makes up 15% of your score. That means the longer you've had credit, the better.

What to do:

Avoid closing old credit cards, even if you don't use them often

Keep them active by making small purchases and paying them off in full

DO NOT close your oldest credit card, it's helping your score

Warning: Many people think *"Oh, I'll just close this credit card since I don't use it"* BAD IDEA. Closing an old account shortens your credit history and can drop your score by 30+ points overnight. Now, if it's a department store credit card, burn it with fire and get rid of it. Those things are financial traps with ridiculously high interest rates.

Stick with one or two solid credit cards with great rewards

Principle #4: Use Credit Responsibly (Strategic Charges plus Military Hacks)

Your credit mix makes up 10% of your score, meaning having different types of credit accounts (credit cards, auto loans, mortgages) can boost your score. BUT, if you aren't budgeting properly, don't use this strategy yet.

Once you have control over your finances, here's a credit-building trick:

Use a **credit card for essential purchases** (gas, groceries, recurring bills)

Pay it off in full every month, so you never pay interest

Earn credit card rewards while improving your score

How I Travel for Free:

I use my American Express Platinum Card for everyday expenses and pay it off in full every month. This lets me:

Earn tons of points for free travel

Get access to luxury airport lounges

Never pay interest while building my credit score

Result? I haven't paid full price for a flight in YEARS.

CREDIT IS YOUR TICKET TO WEALTH

If you master these four credit principles, you'll set yourself up for:

Lower interest rates (saving you thousands)

Easier home buying (better mortgage rates)

More financial opportunities (higher credit limits, better loan approvals)

Remember: Good credit = Money in the bank

Pay your bills on time

Keep your credit balances low

Keep your oldest credit accounts open

Use credit strategically (and take advantage of military perks!)

If you follow these four simple steps, you'll never have to stress over money again.

MILITARY-SPECIFIC CREDIT BENEFITS: YOUR SECRET WEAPON FOR FINANCIAL SECURITY

As a service member, veteran, or military family member, you have access to credit protections and benefits that most civilians could only dream of. These programs exist to help you manage debt, protect your financial well-being, and maximize your benefits, but most service members have no idea they exist! If you're not using these benefits, you're leaving money on the table and making your financial life harder than it needs to be. Let's break it all down.

Servicemembers Civil Relief Act (SCRA) Protections – A Game Changer for Your Finances

The Servicemembers Civil Relief Act (SCRA) is one of the most powerful financial protection laws for military personnel, but many service members don't realize what it covers. Here's what SCRA does for YOU:

Limits Interest Rates to 6% on Pre-Service Debt

- Any loan (credit card, auto, mortgage, personal loan) taken out before joining the military is **capped at 6% interest** while you're on active duty
- This can save you thousands over the life of your loans

Pro Tip: If you have high-interest debt from before your service, contact your lenders and request an SCRA rate adjustment. It's your right, but most lenders won't tell you about it unless you ask.

Protects Against Foreclosure and Eviction

- If you're on active duty and facing financial hardship, SCRA prevents your home from being foreclosed on
- It also stops landlords from evicting you for nonpayment under certain conditions

Allows You to Cancel Leases Without Penalty

- PCS orders? Deployment? You can break your lease (housing, auto, or even cell phone contracts) without financial penalties
- This protection saves thousands of dollars in potential early termination fees

Extends Your Home Sale Tax Exemption by 10 Years!

- Normally, homeowners get a $250,000 tax-free profit ($500,000 for married couples) when selling a primary residence, **IF** they lived there for at least two years within the last five years
- Thanks to SCRA, military members get a **10-YEAR EXTENSION!** That means you can rent out your property for up to thirteen years and still sell it tax-free This is HUGE for building long-term wealth through real estate.

MILITARY-EXCLUSIVE BANKING BENEFITS: LOWER INTEREST RATES & WAIVED FEES

Many banks and credit card companies offer exclusive military benefits to active-duty service members, but you have to ask for them.

Top Credit Cards with No Annual Fees for Active Duty:

- **Amex Platinum** – Normally $695 per year! You get it FREE.
- **Chase Sapphire Reserve** – Normally $550 per year! You get it FREE.
- **Capital One Venture X** – Normally $395 per year! You get it FREE.

Why should you care? These premium travel credit cards come with:

Lounge access at airports worldwide

Free TSA PreCheck & Global Entry ($100 value)

Travel points that can be redeemed for free flights and hotels

Annual travel credits (often $300-$400 per year!)

I personally use my Amex Platinum for all my major purchases and as I mentioned earlier, I haven't paid full price for a flight in years.

How to Get These Fees Waived:

Call your credit card issuer and ask for SCRA benefits

Provide proof of active-duty service (LES or orders)

Enjoy free premium perks while civilians keep paying $500+ per year

Lower Interest Rates on Loans While Deployed

If you deploy to a combat zone, some lenders lower your interest rates even further!

Some credit cards offer 0% APR while deployed (check with your lender)

If you have an auto loan or mortgage, your bank may offer payment deferrals or reduced interest rates

Pro Tip: If you're about to deploy, call your banks and credit card companies and ask what benefits they offer. Some will automatically lower your interest rates, but only if you notify them first.

Struggling with Debt? Use Your Military Resources!

If you're drowning in credit card debt, struggling with bills, or just need financial guidance, don't suffer in silence, there are free resources to help you.

Personal Financial Management Program (PFMP)

- Every military installation has a Personal Financial Counselor who provides free financial coaching

- They help with budgeting, debt reduction, and credit repair

National Foundation for Credit Counseling (NFCC)

- A nonprofit organization that helps military families negotiate with creditors, consolidate debt, and improve credit scores
- Visit **www.nfcc.org** or call **1-800-388-2227** for assistance

Avoid Predatory "Debt Relief" Scams!

- DO NOT fall for scam companies that promise to "erase your debt" or "fix your credit overnight"
- Many charge insane fees for things you can do for free with PFMP or NFCC

FINAL THOUGHTS: TAKE CONTROL OF YOUR CREDIT

Your credit score is one of the most powerful financial tools you have. By following these foundational principles, you can maintain a strong credit score, reduce financial stress, and access better financial opportunities.

The Five Key Components of Your Credit Score:

- **Payment History – 35%**
- This is the most important factor. Missed payments hurt your score more than anything else.
- **Amounts Owed (Utilization) – 30%**
- Keep your balances low relative to your total credit limits. Ideally, use less than 30% of your available credit.
- **Length of Credit History – 15%**
- The longer your accounts have been open, the better. Don't close old credit cards unless absolutely necessary.
- **New Credit – 10%**

- Too many recent applications for credit can signal risk. Be selective when applying for new accounts.
- **Credit Mix – 10%**
- A healthy mix of installment loans (like auto loans) and revolving credit (like credit cards) helps your score.

Four Credit Habits for Success:

- **Pay all bills on time** – Set up automatic payments to avoid missed due dates.
- **Keep credit balances low** – Aim for under 30% of your total available credit.
- **Keep old accounts open** – A long credit history builds trust with lenders.
- **Use credit wisely** – Borrow only what you can repay. Don't overextend yourself.

Understanding military-specific credit protections can also save you thousands of dollars and help you avoid financial pitfalls. Tools like the Servicemembers Civil Relief Act (SCRA) can reduce interest rates and protect your financial standing during service. Take advantage of every benefit available and treat your credit score like a mission-critical asset.

I hear and forget. What I write I understand.

FIVE
LEVERAGING COMPOUND INTEREST

"COMPOUND INTEREST IS THE EIGHTH WONDER OF THE WORLD. HE WHO UNDERSTANDS IT, EARNS IT... HE WHO DOESN'T, PAYS IT."

– Albert Einstein

WHEN IT COMES TO MONEY, there are two kinds of people in this world: those who understand how interest works for them and those who suffer because it works against them. The difference is staggering. Those who harness compound interest build wealth effortlessly, while those who don't find themselves drowning in debt that never seems to go away.

Think of compound interest like a snowball rolling down a hill. If you start rolling it early, it picks up more snow and grows exponentially. But if you wait until the bottom of the hill to start, the snowball barely has time to grow. That's exactly how money works; the sooner you start, the bigger your returns will be.

This is why the most common financial regret people have is not investing earlier. I've met countless people in their forties and fifties who say, *"I wish I had started saving and investing in my twenties."* Why? Because once they finally understood the power of compound interest, they realized how much money they could have had if they had started earlier.

If you invest just $100 per month starting at age twenty, you could have over $1 million by retirement

If you wait until age forty to start investing, you would have to invest $600 per month to reach the same goal

If you wait until age fifty? You'd have to invest nearly $2,000 per month.

See the problem? You can't make up for lost time. Time is the single most important factor in growing wealth. But here's the kicker: compound interest doesn't care about your excuses. It doesn't care if you "forgot to start early" or if you "didn't know any better." It rewards those who take action and punishes those who wait.

This chapter will break down how interest affects your financial future, why investing early is a game-changer, and when you should focus on paying off debt versus investing. Whether you're just starting out or playing catch-up, it's never too late to make compound interest work in your favor. The key is to take action now.

HOW INTEREST WORKS FOR AND AGAINST YOU

Interest is a double-edged sword: it can either help you build wealth or keep you drowning in debt. The way you use interest will determine whether you're in control of your finances or being controlled by them.

When Interest Works Against You: The Debt Trap

If you carry a balance on a credit card or take out high-interest loans, compound interest is your enemy. Credit card companies make billions of dollars because they understand how interest accumulates over time, and they bank on the fact that most people don't.

Think of it this way: if you use a credit card the wrong way, you're not just paying for what you bought, you're paying for it multiple times thanks to interest.

Example of How Debt Grows:

- You have a $5,000 balance on a credit card with a 22% interest rate
- You only make the minimum payment each month
- It will take over twenty years to pay off that debt, and you'll end up paying more than $10,000 in interest alone!

That means you could have bought that item twice, maybe even three times, by the time you finish paying it off. Ever wonder why credit card companies push "minimum payments" so hard? Because if you only pay the minimum, they win and you lose. The majority of that payment goes toward interest, not your actual balance. It's like throwing money into a black hole.

And it's not just credit cards: payday loans, car loans with insane interest rates, and predatory personal loans are all designed to trap you in a cycle of debt. That's why paying off high-interest debt should be a top priority before focusing on major investments. Otherwise, your investments will never outpace your debt.

When Interest Works for You: Investment Growth

On the flip side, compound interest can work in your favor when you invest. The earlier you start investing, the more time your money has to grow, and time is the secret weapon of every wealthy investor. Imagine if, instead of paying thousands in credit card interest, you were earning thousands from investments instead.

Example of How Investing Grows:

- You invest $5,000 in an account that earns an 8% annual return

- Instead of withdrawing, you reinvest your earnings
- In twenty years, that same $5,000 becomes over $23,000
- In forty years, it grows to $109,000!

Now think about that credit card example again. Would you rather be paying thousands in interest or earning thousands in interest? This is the exact same principle that makes credit card companies rich, except now, you are the one profiting. The lesson here? Master interest before it masters you. If you're in debt, make paying it off a mission priority. If you're debt-free, start making compound interest work for you as soon as possible. Because the longer you wait, the more you're leaving on the table.

THE STORY OF TRAVIS & SEBASTIAN – A LESSON IN INVESTING EARLY

Investing early is like planting a tree: the sooner you plant it, the larger, stronger, and more valuable it will grow over time. Just like a tree takes years to develop deep roots and a strong trunk, your investments need time to maximize their growth through compound interest.

Many people delay investing because they believe they need a large amount of money to start. That's a myth. Time in the market beats timing the market. The most critical factor in wealth-building isn't how much you invest—it's when you start.

The Story of Travis & Sebastian

Let's break it down using a real-world example, one that hits close to home for me. Yes, this is a true story of my son, Sebastian and I. Sebastian started investing early at nineteen and contributed a modest amount every month. I, on the other hand, waited until my mid-thirties to start investing seriously, but I contributed far more each month than Sebastian. Even though I invested significantly more overall, Sebastian is on track to have more money by retirement than I ever will.

Wait, what? How is that possible? It all comes down to compound interest.

Sebastian had one major advantage: TIME. Because his money was invested for a longer period, it had more time to compound and grow exponentially. Meanwhile, even though I contributed far more money overall, my investments had a shorter time horizon and didn't benefit from as many compounding cycles.

Key Takeaways from Travis & Sebastian's Story:

Starting early allows compound interest to do the heavy lifting

The earlier you start, the less money you need to contribute to reach the same financial goal.

Even small amounts invested early outperform larger amounts invested later

If Sebastian had only invested $200 per month from twenty-one to thirty, his investment still would have outperformed my $500 per month starting in my mid-thirties.

The longer you wait, the harder it is to catch up

If you delay investing, you'll have to contribute significantly more money to reach the same level of financial security.

Think of investing like fitness

If you start working out in your early twenties, it's easier to maintain a strong, healthy body later in life. But if you wait until your forties or fifties to get in shape, you'll have to work twice as hard to achieve the same results. The same goes for money: start early, and let time work in your favor.

Let's break this down if to an even playing field between Travis and Sebastian:

If **Sebastian** invested $2,400 annually from age nineteen to thirty, totaling **$26,400**, then let it grow untouched.

And if **Travis** invested $2,400 annually from age thirty to sixty-seven, totaling **$88,800**.

Despite contributing significantly less, **Sebastian ends up with over $3.67 million**, more than **double** Travis's **$1.46 million**.

The Bottom Line: Just Start

There is never a perfect time to invest, but the worst thing you can do is keep waiting. Even if you can only afford $50 a month right now, start investing. The habit matters more than the amount. Over time, you can increase your contributions as a percentage of your income as your income grows.

Sebastian's story proves that small, consistent investments made early can lead to massive financial success later in life. So, if you're reading this and haven't started yet, start today. Your future self will thank you.

MY PERSONAL JOURNEY WITH COMPOUND INTEREST

I didn't quite understand the power of compound interest for the longest time. As a matter of fact, I was a very late bloomer when it came to investing. I didn't learn about the power of compound interest investing until I was in my mid-thirties, so I've been playing catch-up ever since. In this analogy of Travis and Sebastian, I was basically Travis, a late bloomer who had to scramble to make up for lost time.

Understanding that time is not your friend when it comes to investing and grasping the **Rule of** 7 (where your money doubles every seven years at a decent return rate) was a game-changer for me. If I hadn't figured this out, I'd still be scraping by, living paycheck to paycheck.

After twenty-four years in the Navy, I did have my **TSP**, but I realized that once I left the military, I could no longer contribute to it unless I transitioned into a government job. This meant I had to roll my TSP funds into higher-yield investments that would take full advantage of compound interest. There are many different investment vehicles available and understanding them is key to building long-term wealth. I'll cover those later, but for now, know this: start as early as you can and leverage compound interest to your advantage.

DEBT VS. INVESTING: WHICH SHOULD YOU PRIORITIZE?

One of the biggest financial dilemmas people face is deciding between paying off debt and investing for the future. The answer? It depends on the type of debt and interest rates, but the worst mistake you can make is doing nothing.

A common misconception is that investing should always come first because of compound interest. While investing early is crucial, there's one problem: high-interest debt will eat away at your financial gains faster than your investments can grow. If you're earning an 8% return in the stock market but paying 22% interest on a credit card, you're actually losing money.

This is why financial freedom starts with eliminating bad debt before aggressively investing. Otherwise, it's like trying to run a marathon with ankle weights; you're moving forward, but not nearly as fast as you could be.

When to Prioritize Paying Off Debt First:

If any of the following applies to you, it's time to attack your debt before focusing on long-term investing:

Your debt carries an interest rate of 6% or higher. Credit cards, personal loans, payday loans, and high-interest car loans are financial quicksand. Paying them off guarantees you a "return" equal to the interest rate you're eliminating.

Your debt has a variable interest rate. Adjustable-rate loans can increase over time, making them an unpredictable financial burden. If rates spike, your payments can skyrocket, leaving you scrambling.

Your debt is causing financial stress. If your monthly payments are eating up your cash flow, keeping you up at night, or preventing you from covering necessities, prioritize eliminating that stress. Financial peace of mind is invaluable.

Your minimum payments aren't making a dent. If you're stuck in a cycle of only paying interest while the principal barely moves, you'll never get ahead. High-interest debt needs to be wiped out as quickly as possible.

When to Prioritize Investing First:

Once you've tamed your high-interest debt, it's time to shift your focus to building wealth. Here's when investing should take priority:

You have low-interest debt (under 5%). Mortgages, federal student loans, and other low-interest debts don't need to be rushed. Instead, use your extra money to invest where it can generate higher returns.

Your employer offers a 401(k) match. This is free money! If your company matches contributions, always take full advantage; it's an immediate 100% return on your investment.

Your investments are expected to grow at a higher rate than your debt interest. If your debt carries a 3% interest rate but you can earn 8% investing, it makes sense to let your money grow rather than aggressively paying off cheap debt.

The Hybrid Approach: Balance Is Key

For most people, the best strategy is a mix of both: paying down debt while simultaneously investing. This allows you to reduce financial stress while still taking advantage of compounding returns.

Example: If you have an extra $500 per month, you could allocate $300 toward high-interest debt and $200 toward investing. Once the debt is gone, that full $500 can then be directed toward wealth-building investments.

The key takeaway? **Don't ignore one in favor of the other.** Pay off toxic debt, take advantage of investment opportunities, and create a financial strategy that puts you in control.

FINAL THOUGHTS: MAKE COMPOUND INTEREST WORK FOR YOU

- **Avoid high-interest debt**: it will destroy your financial future
- **Start investing early**: time in the market beats timing the market
- **Balance debt repayment and investing**: find what works for your situation
- **Leverage OPM (Other People's Money) wisely**: use good debt to build assets, not liabilities

I hear and forget. What I write I understand.

SIX
MILITARY INVESTMENT VEHICLES

"THE STOCK MARKET IS DESIGNED TO TRANSFER MONEY FROM THE ACTIVE TO THE PATIENT."

~ ***Warren Buffett***

I DIDN'T FULLY UNDERSTAND this quote when I first started exploring the world of investing. Like many service members, I was focused on the immediate: making sure I had enough to pay my bills, put food on the table, and maybe have a little left over for a night out. The idea of putting money away for decades just didn't seem relevant at the time. But the truth is, patience in investing is what separates those who build wealth from those who never escape the paycheck-to-paycheck cycle.

As a service member, veteran, or military family member, you have unique opportunities to build wealth through investment vehicles tailored for the military community. These aren't just generic options that apply to the general public; there are specific benefits and programs available only to those who have served. If you take the time to understand and use them properly, these tools can provide financial stability, long-term security, and ultimately financial freedom.

One of the biggest mistakes I see veterans and military personnel make is thinking they don't earn enough to invest or that investing is only for the rich. That couldn't be further from the truth. Investing isn't about how much money you have; it's about how much time you give your money to grow.

Like the story of my son and I, let me give you a real-world example: imagine two military members, Private Early and Sergeant Late (I just made these names up, but bear with me). Private Early starts investing just $100 a month at age twenty. Sergeant Late waits until he's forty and starts investing $500 a month. Fast forward to age sixty-five, and despite Sergeant Late investing five times as much per month, he still ends up with less money because Private Early let time and compound interest do the work.

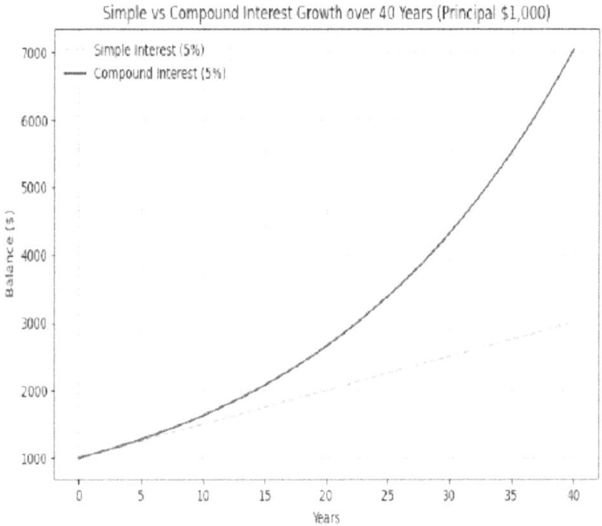

In this chapter, we'll cover three major categories of investments available to military personnel and veterans:

1. **TSP** – The military's version of a 401(k) with Traditional and Roth options

2. **Index Funds, Stocks, and Bonds** – Low-cost investments for sustainable wealth growth
3. **Alternative Investments** – Exploring modern investing trends, from crypto to automated investing apps

However, before diving into these, I want to make a disclaimer: **I am not a financial advisor**. Everything I provide here is based on my personal experience and knowledge. I highly encourage you to consult a fiduciary financial advisor, and I again emphasize **fiduciary** because that means they are legally obligated to make investment decisions in your best interest rather than lining their own pockets. Too many so-called "financial advisors" are really just glorified salespeople pushing high-fee products that benefit them more than you. Don't fall into that trap.

I also want to address a common misconception in the military community; many service members think that the government or the VA is going to "take care of them" in retirement. Yes, there are benefits like pensions and disability, but those alone are NOT enough to build wealth. If you want to live comfortably, travel, and not worry about money when you retire, you need to start thinking beyond your military paycheck.

The key takeaway here: The stock market isn't about getting rich quickly, it's about getting rich slowly and securely. If you approach investing with the right mindset and strategy, your future self will thank you. Now, let's break down exactly how you can leverage these investment vehicles to maximize your financial potential.

THE IMPORTANCE OF DIVERSIFICATION

One of the most critical principles of investing is **diversification**. There's a reason why every financial expert, book, and overly enthusiastic dude at the bar who just discovered investing will tell you, "Don't put all your eggs in one basket." Because if that one investment goes belly-up, you're not just losing money, you're losing all of it. Instead, you want to spread your investments across different vehicles, balancing risk and reward to keep yourself financially secure.

Short-Term Investments – Cash reserves, high-yield savings accounts, and short-term bonds. Think of these as your oh-crap fund, things that keep your money liquid and accessible in case of an emergency.

Mid-Term Investments – Index funds, ETFs, and dividend stocks. These grow your wealth at a solid, predictable rate while still allowing flexibility.

Long-Term Investments – Retirement accounts like TSP, Roth IRAs, real estate, and whole life insurance policies with cash value. These are for future you—the one who wants to enjoy life and not work at Walmart as a greeter in retirement.

Speculative Investments – Cryptocurrency, NFTs, venture capital, and startup companies, etc... This is your YOLO money: high risk, high reward, and only invest what you're prepared to lose (seriously, don't bet your mortgage on Dogecoin).

WHY DIVERSIFICATION IS NON-NEGOTIABLE

I learned this lesson the hard way. Back in the day, I thought I was being smart when I dumped a huge chunk of money into one stock that I was convinced was going to the moon. I did my "research" (which consisted of a five-minute Reddit thread), and I was so sure I was going to double my money in weeks. Fast forward a few months, and that stock tanked hard. I didn't just lose money; I lost my confidence in investing for a while. That's when I learned the golden rule: Never put all your faith (or cash) into one investment.

You don't want to be the guy who bets everything on the latest stock tip, only to wake up and realize your "sure thing" has plummeted 80% overnight. It's like going all-in on a blind date—you're either meeting your future spouse, or you're getting ghosted after paying for an expensive steak dinner. The true key to investment success is diversity and steady, long-term growth with an 8-12% return. That's not sexy, but it works.

"But I Can't Afford to Invest Right Now" – Lies We Tell Ourselves

Now, let's be real. I know what you're thinking: "This all sounds great, but I barely have enough to cover my Netflix subscription, let alone diversify my investments." Trust me, I get it. I used to think investing was only for rich people, you know, the guys in tailored suits who say things like "I'll have my assistant handle that," and own yachts with names like *Serenity*. But here's the thing; even small investments add up over time.

That $5 you spend on a Starbucks coffee every morning? If you invested that in an S&P 500 index fund instead, you'd have over $75,000 in thirty years. That's a hell of a lot of caramel macchiatos you're trading in for financial security. So next time you think you "can't afford to invest," ask yourself if you can afford not to. Because if you don't start now, future you is going to be looking back in twenty years wondering why you didn't make small sacrifices for a much bigger reward.

Don't Fall for the Hype

Another rookie mistake? Chasing trends. If you're hearing about an investment on the news, it's probably too late. Take GameStop, for example. The moment that became a mainstream story, people flooded in hoping to strike it rich. The ones who made real money? The ones who got in before it became a meme. The ones who jumped in late? Well, they paid for the ones who cashed out.

The key to investing isn't chasing the next big thing; it's slow, steady, and consistent growth. The stock market isn't a casino, and if you treat it like one, you're going to end up broke.

"I skate to where the puck is going to be, not where it has been."- Wayne Gretzky

This is a great quote to think about when you are considering investing. Just remember, if a hot stock makes it to the news, it's too f#(king late, you missed it!

HOW TO KEEP YOUR COOL IN A MARKET MELTDOWN

Another common mistake investors make is panicking during market downturns. It's easy to feel like the sky is falling when your portfolio suddenly looks like a crime scene. But here's a secret: the best investors don't run from the fire, they run toward it. When the market dips, that's when stocks go on sale. If Apple or Tesla stock suddenly dropped by 30%, you'd be getting a huge discount, so why would you run away?

Imagine walking into Best Buy and seeing TVs are suddenly 50% off. Would you run out of the store screaming, or would you buy a TV? The stock market works the same way: buy when it's low, hold, and wait for it to go back up. The biggest wealth transfers in history have happened during recessions. Those who held steady and kept investing ended up making serious money when the market rebounded. Those who panicked and pulled out? They locked in their losses.

Remember: It's not about timing the market. It's about time in the market. The longer you stay invested, the better your chances of success.

Invest Smart, Stay Diversified, and Don't Freak Out

Investing doesn't have to be scary or complicated, if you just stick to these simple rules:

Diversify your investments: don't put all your eggs in one basket

Start investing now: even small amounts make a big difference over time

Ignore media hype: if it's in the news, you're already too late

Stay calm during downturns: smart investors buy when everyone else is panicking

And most importantly…**don't bet the farm on Dogecoin.**

THE THRIFT SAVINGS PLAN (TSP): MILITARY RETIREMENT SAVINGS

If you're in the military and not contributing to the TSP, you're leaving money on the table. The TSP is the government's version of a 401(k) and is one of the easiest ways for service members to save for retirement.

Traditional vs. Roth TSP: What's the Difference?

Feature

Traditional TSP

Roth TSP

Taxes on Contributions

Tax-deferred (reduces taxable income now)

Taxed upfront (no tax deduction now)

Taxes on Withdrawals

Fully taxed as ordinary income at retirement

Tax-free withdrawals in retirement (if eligible)

Best for:

Those expecting a lower tax rate in retirement

Those who believe taxes will be higher in the future

- **Traditional TSP** is great if you want to **reduce your taxable income now** and expect a lower tax bracket in retirement.
- **Roth TSP** is ideal if you want to **pay taxes upfront** and enjoy **tax-free growth** for life.

Important Note: Once you leave the military, you can no longer contribute to the TSP unless you transition into a government job. However, you can roll your TSP into a higher-yield investment account to continue growing your money effectively.

I'll be honest, when I first started contributing to my TSP, I had no idea what I was doing. I just picked some random funds, hoping for the best. I later realized that choosing the right funds can make a HUGE difference. Imagine two service members retire after twenty years; one took full advantage of the C and S funds, while the other played it safe in the G fund. The first one is sipping margaritas on a beach in retirement; the second one is still clipping coupons at the commissary. Be the margarita guy.

ALTERNATIVE INVESTMENTS: THINKING OUTSIDE THE BOX

Beyond traditional stocks and bonds, alternative investments offer new ways to build wealth. These investments come with higher risk, but they also have the potential for higher rewards, or, if you're not careful, a one-way ticket to Brokeville.

Now, I've always been a bit skeptical about the so-called "next big thing" in investing. If I had a dollar for every time someone tried to get me into the latest "foolproof" money-making opportunity, I probably wouldn't need to invest at all. From multi-level marketing schemes to day-trading penny stocks, I've seen enough "sure things" turn into disasters to know that chasing trends is a dangerous game.

But that doesn't mean all alternative investments are bad. Some have real potential, if you approach them wisely, diversify properly, and don't dump all your money into a single bet.

Cryptocurrency: The Wild West of Investing

Cryptocurrency is one of the most controversial investment vehicles today. Coins like **Bitcoin (BTC)** and **Ethereum (ETH)** have seen explosive growth, but they are also highly volatile. If the stock market is like a roller coaster, crypto is like strapping yourself to a bottle rocket and hoping for the best.

I remember when Bitcoin was just a few hundred bucks. A buddy of mine tried to get me to buy some, and I laughed in his face. "You want me to invest in fake internet money?" Fast forward a few years, and that same buddy was driving a brand-new Tesla while I was still questioning my life choices. Lesson learned.

But here's the thing about crypto—for every person who "made it," there are dozens more who got wrecked. Some people threw their life savings into Dogecoin, thinking it was going "to the moon," only to watch it crash back to Earth faster than a SpaceX test flight gone wrong. Crypto had massive price swings, and people who went all-in on it without diversifying saw their portfolios drop drastically during downturns. Some have recovered, but many lost thousands, if not millions, of dollars.

The biggest mistake? Buying high and panic-selling low. When Bitcoin was at $60,000, everyone wanted in. When it crashed to $20,000, people ran for the exits. That's the exact opposite of what you should do. Invest wisely, don't overcommit, and for the love of all that is holy, don't invest money you can't afford to lose.

NFTs: Digital Gold or Fool's Gold?

Ah, **NFTs (Non-Fungible Tokens),** perhaps the wildest of all alternative investments. At one point, people were dropping millions on digital pictures of cartoon apes and pixelated punks. Why? I have no idea.

One of my friends tried to convince me to buy an NFT, and when I asked him why I should pay thousands for a JPEG, he hit me with, "But bro, it's on the blockchain." That's when I knew we were living in crazy times.

Now, I'm not saying NFTs are all scams, but let's be real, most of them are. A lot of people jumped into NFTs thinking they were the next Bitcoin, only to realize that hype alone doesn't create value.

Can NFTs be valuable? Sure. But are most of them worthless now? Also, yes. If you're going to dabble in NFTs, treat them like art collecting; only buy what you genuinely think has value, and don't expect to flip it for millions overnight.

Venture Capital & Startups: High-Risk, High-Reward

Investing in startups or private companies can yield massive returns if successful. However, most startups fail, so this is a high-risk strategy.

- **Angel Investing** – Providing capital to early-stage companies
- **Crowdfunding Platforms** – Sites like **SeedInvest** or **Republic** allow everyday investors to fund startups

I once had a buddy who was convinced he had the next billion-dollar idea. He pitched it to me over drinks, and I'll admit, his enthusiasm was contagious. But when I asked him how he planned to actually make money, he just stared at me blankly and said, "We'll figure that out later." That's when I knew it was a hard pass.

Look, venture capital is not for the faint of heart. If you're going to invest in startups, make sure you understand the risks and only invest money you're willing to lose.

AUTOMATED INVESTING APPS: SET IT AND FORGET IT

If you're new to investing and don't know where to start, automated investing apps like **Acorns**, **Robinhood**, and **M1 Finance** can help. These apps simplify investing by automating deposits and investments based on your goals.

- **Acorns** – Rounds up spare change from purchases and invests it

- **Robinhood** – Commission-free trading for stocks and crypto
- **M1 Finance** – Automates investing into portfolios based on your goals

Now, I used to think these apps were a gimmick. But after seeing how easy they make investing, I have changed my tune. If setting up a brokerage account feels overwhelming, these apps make it as easy as ordering food on DoorDash.

That said, be careful with apps like Robinhood, because they make trading way too easy. If you're not careful, you'll wake up at 3AM, see a Reddit post about some random stock, and before you know it, you've dumped your entire paycheck into a company you've never even heard of. I know because I've been there.

FINAL THOUGHTS: ALTERNATIVE INVESTMENTS CAN WORK—IF YOU'RE SMART

Alternative investments can be exciting, profitable, and sometimes life-changing. But they can also be dangerous if you don't do your homework. Just remember to follow the **Golden Rule:**

- **Diversify** – Never put all your money into one thing
- **Do Your Research** – If you don't understand how an investment makes money, don't invest
- **Don't Buy Hype** – If it's on the news, it's too late
- **Only Invest What You Can Afford to Lose** – If an investment goes to zero, you should still be okay

Remember, investing isn't about getting rich quick, it's about getting rich smart. If you keep that in mind, you'll be miles ahead of the guy betting his mortgage on the next meme coin.

Build Your Investment Strategy

Investing is not a one-size-fits-all approach. The key is to diversify, align investments with your financial goals, and understanding your risk tolerance.

TSP – A must-have for military members, especially if you qualify for a **5% match** under the Blended Retirement System

Index Funds & Stocks – The best long-term investment strategy for wealth building

Alternative Investments – Can supplement your portfolio, but approach with caution

Don't panic sell – Market dips are buying opportunities, not reasons to flee.

I hear and forget. What I write I understand.

SEVEN
MILITARY BENEFITS THAT BUILD WEALTH

LEVERAGING MILITARY BENEFITS FOR LONG-TERM FINANCIAL SUCCESS

ONE OF THE biggest mistakes I see service members and veterans make is not fully utilizing the financial benefits the military provides. The military offers some of the most powerful wealth-building tools available, but too many people either don't know how to use them or don't think long-term about their impact. If you play your cards right, you can set yourself up for financial success, homeownership, and career growth, without massive debt

I've seen too many fellow service members waste these benefits by not knowing how powerful they are. Some think, "I'll figure it out later," and then later never comes. Others use their benefits without a plan, kind of like the guy who blows his reenlistment bonus on a brand-new car and then suddenly realizes he still has rent, bills, and child support to pay. Don't be that guy. I knew a guy who got a fat bonus, took one look at his bank account, and said, "I'm rich, baby!" Next thing you know, he had chrome rims, a PlayStation 5, and a 75-inch

TV, but somehow, no groceries and no gas money. A month later, he was borrowing money for food. That's not wealth-building, that's just a financial face plant.

The thing is, most military benefits aren't just short-term perks; they're designed to set you up for life if you use them wisely. However, no one really sits down and teaches us this stuff. You get handed a stack of paperwork when you enlist and buried somewhere between the SGLI life insurance form and the "don't do anything stupid" speech, there's some fine print about the GI Bill, BAH, and VA Home Loans, but it's up to you to actually use them correctly.

Think of it like this: if someone handed you a free toolbox, but you never learned how to use the tools, that's on you. These benefits are your financial toolbox, but if you let them sit in the corner collecting dust, you're missing out on tens (or even hundreds) of thousands of dollars.

In this chapter, we're going to break down three of the most valuable military benefits and how to leverage them to build wealth, not just survive. We'll go over:

1. **GI Bill & Education Benefits** – How to use them wisely for career growth
2. **Military Housing Allowances (BAH)** – How to turn housing benefits into financial gain
3. **VA Home Loans & Homeownership** – Building equity instead of throwing money away on rent

. . .

If you take these seriously, you can walk away from military service not just with a DD-214 and some cool war stories, but with real financial security. Because, let's be honest, you don't want to be the 50-year-old guy still living paycheck to paycheck, talking about how you "should've invested" your BAH.

GI BILL & EDUCATION BENEFITS – YOUR TICKET TO CAREER GROWTH

If you don't take full advantage of your GI Bill, you're leaving tens of thousands of dollars on the table, possibly more. Education is one of the most expensive investments civilians make, yet the military hands you a way to get it for free, if you use it wisely.

Post-9/11 GI Bill vs. Montgomery GI Bill

Feature

Post-9/11 GI Bill

Montgomery GI Bill

Tuition Coverage

Full tuition for public schools, up to a cap for private schools

Monthly stipend for tuition and expenses

Housing Allowance

BAH at E-5 with dependents rate

None

Book Stipend

Up to $1,000 per year

None

Transfer Benefits

Can transfer to spouse or children

No transfer option

- **Best Option**: For most people, the Post-9/11 GI Bill is the best choice because it covers full tuition, housing, and books.
- **Montgomery GI Bill** can be useful if you just need a small tuition stipend while using other military benefits.

MAXIMIZING YOUR GI BILL

Too many people waste their GI Bill on degrees that don't lead to high-paying careers. I'm not saying you shouldn't study what you love, but let's be real, if you're using your GI Bill to get a degree in underwater basket weaving, don't be surprised when you're struggling to find a job later.

I knew a guy who used his GI Bill to get a degree in philosophy. Now, don't get me wrong, understanding the meaning of life is great and all, but the only people making money off philosophy are college professors and self-help book authors. Meanwhile, my buddy in cybersecurity who used his GI Bill for a few certifications is now making six figures. **Choose wisely.**

Pro Tip: Use your GI Bill for in-demand careers like IT, cybersecurity, engineering, healthcare, and skilled trades. These fields pay well and have job security—meaning you'll get the best return on investment (ROI) for your free education.

Even better? You can use your GI Bill for trade schools, certifications, and SkillBridge programs, not just traditional college. If a four-year degree isn't your thing, you can still use it to get a high-paying certification in tech, real estate, or project management.

And here's something many veterans don't realize: my company (and others like mine), **Military Operated Real Estate (MORE),** offers an apprenticeship program in California which is an incredible way to leverage your veteran education benefits to get hands-on training in real estate while earning an income. Since it's VA-approved, it allows eligible veterans to receive a housing stipend while gaining practical skills in the real estate industry. So, if you're looking for a career path that doesn't require sitting in a classroom for four years but still offers serious earning potential, this is a game-changer worth considering.

The key takeaway? **Your GI Bill is one of the most powerful tools you have. Use it wisely and it will pay dividends for the rest of your life.**

MILITARY HOUSING ALLOWANCES – HOW TO TURN BAH INTO AN INVESTMENT

BAH is one of the most underrated financial tools available to military personnel. The problem? Most people blow it on expensive rentals instead of using it to build wealth.

Option 1: Buying a Home and Keeping the Equity

If you're stationed somewhere for at least three years, consider buying a home instead of renting. With a VA Home Loan (which we'll cover next), you can buy with zero down, and your BAH can cover your mortgage. This is how many veterans start building real estate portfolios while still serving, by turning their first home into a rental when they PCS and repeating the process at their next duty station.

I know a guy who lived off ramen noodles so he could buy a fourplex with a VA Home Loan, live in one unit, and rent out the others. His tenants paid his mortgage, and he used his BAH to stack cash and invest. He retired from the military with a real estate empire while some of us were still debating whether to lease a new Dodge Charger at 20% interest. That's called playing the game smart.

Option 2: Investing the BAH You Don't Use

Not ready to buy a home? You can still use your BAH to build wealth. Instead of renting an expensive luxury apartment that eats up your entire housing allowance, consider renting below your means and investing the leftover BAH.

Here's how you can make it work:

- If your BAH is $2,500/month, but you rent for $1,800, you now have $700 left over each month.
- Instead of spending that money, you could invest it into an S&P 500 index fund, which has historically returned 8-12% annually.
- Over twenty years, that $700/month could grow to over $500,000—just from investing your leftover housing allowance.

Alternatively, you can **diversify your investments**:

Real Estate Crowdfunding – Platforms like Fundrise or REITs allow you to invest in real estate without buying property

Dividend Stocks – Invest in companies that **pay you passive income** through quarterly dividends

Cryptocurrency (if you like risk) – Set aside a small portion of your BAH to invest in blue-chip cryptos like Bitcoin or Ethereum, but only what you can afford to lose

The key here is discipline; don't let the extra cash burn a hole in your pocket. Just because you can afford a luxury apartment with rooftop pools and a concierge doesn't mean you should.

Think long-term: Would you rather have a fancy apartment now or half a million dollars invested when you retire? I know what I'd pick.

VA HOME LOANS & HOMEOWNERSHIP – STOP THROWING MONEY AWAY ON RENT

The **VA Home Loan** is one of the best home-buying benefits available to veterans, but many people don't use it correctly or don't use it at all.

Why VA Home Loans Are a Game Changer

- **No Down Payment** – you don't need 20% down like civilians do
- **No Private Mortgage Insurance (PMI)** – saves you hundreds per month
- **Lower Interest Rates** – VA Home Loans typically have better rates than traditional mortgages
- **Easier Qualification** – the VA backs the loan, making it easier to get approved

How to Use a VA Home Loan the Right Way

Too many service members buy too much house and end up house-poor. Just because you qualify for a $500,000 loan doesn't mean you should spend that much. Instead, use these smart strategies:

Buy a home you can afford –just because the VA lets you buy zero down doesn't mean you should max out your loan

Look for homes in growing areas – areas with good rental potential if you need to move

Turn your home into an investment – plan to rent it out when you PCS

FINAL THOUGHTS: MILITARY BENEFITS ARE A PATH TO WEALTH—IF YOU USE THEM WISELY

- **Use your GI Bill strategically** – pick a high-ROI career path instead of wasting it
- **Leverage BAH** – invest in property or live below your means and invest the extra cash
- **VA Home Loans are powerful** – use them wisely to build equity and wealth, not just buy a flashy home

Many people leave the military with nothing to show financially—but you don't have to. By using these benefits the right way, you can set yourself up for lifelong financial success while still serving your country.

I hear and forget. What I write I understand.

EIGHT
THE VA HOME LOAN ADVANTAGE

MY FIRST HOME PURCHASE – A HARD LESSON LEARNED

HERE'S my story about the first time I bought a home and did not use my VA home loan. In the early 2000s, and I was stationed in Virginia when I decided to buy my very first home. At the time, I had a Realtor who clearly didn't understand the value of the VA home loan benefit, so he convinced me to go with a conventional loan instead.

Now, let's set the scene: this was the wild wild west of lending, where subprime mortgages, stated income loans, adjustable-rate mortgages (ARMs), and interest-only loans were being handed out like candy. And as a young and financially uneducated Sailor, I got sucked right into it.

The home was priced at $125,000, and my Realtor (along with a very eager loan officer) convinced me that an interest-only ARM was the way to go. My monthly mortgage payment would only be $400, and I thought, *"Hell yeah! I can afford that!"* No one ever told me what an ARM actually meant or what would happen when the rates adjusted.

Fast forward one year later, and that "sweet" 2% interest rate vanished overnight. Suddenly, my mortgage shot up to 8%, and my payment literally tripled. And do you think I, a young Sailor living paycheck to paycheck with so much debt, had factored that into my budget? Hell no. Suddenly, I was struggling to survive, living off ramen, stretching my paychecks, and damn near qualifying for food stamps.

But, by pure luck and timing, I received orders to transfer overseas and had the opportunity to sell my home before the real estate market collapsed. In December 2005, I listed my house for just over $200,000, and while we had zero traction at first, I eventually dropped the price to $199,000 and got an offer. We closed escrow in January 2006, and this is not an exaggeration; three weeks later, the real estate market crashed.

I had friends who listed their homes just a month after I sold mine, and they couldn't sell at all. They had to drop their prices by 50%, 60%, or even 70% just to get buyers interested. Meanwhile, I was watching the housing market implode from the safety of my new duty station overseas. I got incredibly lucky.

But that hard lesson stuck with me. I learned firsthand what happens when you don't fully understand your loan options and when you trust the wrong people to guide you.

MY SECOND HOME PURCHASE – THE RIGHT WAY TO BUY WITH A VA HOME LOAN

My second experience purchasing a home was in 2009 after I got orders to come to California. After my first experience, I was a little gun shy, but I knew that owning a home was much better than renting. The first agent I used to help me find a home while I was stationed overseas was a civilian. While he may have been a decent real estate agent, he did not understand the unique challenges of military life, and he definitely didn't know what it felt like to be disconnected while stationed overseas. He was not responsive, and he kept steering me away from short sales, which made up about 90% of the listings in 2009.

I was frustrated. I knew that buying a home in a market that was still recovering from the crash would set me up for long-term financial success, but I needed someone who actually understood my situation. That's when I was referred to an active-duty officer in real estate, Derek.

Derek would later become the catalyst for me getting into real estate, but at the time, he was simply the right person at the right time. He knew exactly what I needed as a military buyer and how to leverage all the benefits afforded to me, including my VA Home Loan.

I'll never forget how he went above and beyond; he literally picked me up from the airport when I flew in to house hunt and drove me around for a week to find the right home. If you ask him, he'd probably tell you I was his most demanding client, and he'd be right! I had a million questions, and I wanted everything to be perfect.

But despite my relentless questioning, Derek made the process seamless because he understood the challenges of being in the military. He showed me exactly how the home-buying experience should be for veterans, and it completely changed my perspective. Without his guidance, I don't know how my experience would have turned out, but one thing's for sure, he set the standard for how veterans should be taken care of in real estate. That experience inspired me to get into real estate myself, and Derek remains a friend and mentor to this day. I am truly grateful.

Another important lesson I learned? Understanding values. When I was looking at homes in 2009, I was sticker-shocked by the prices. A three-bedroom, two-bath home, 1,700 square feet was going for over $300,000. My immediate thought? Why would I spend $300,000 on a house when my first home only cost $125,000? Derek broke it down for me in a way that completely shifted my mindset:

"Would you rather have $100,000 in the bank or $300,000 in the bank when you pay off the loan or go to sell?"

The bottom line? As long as your income matches the housing market, you should always consider purchasing. Because at the end of the day, equity is what matters. Owning real estate in California, where property values appreciate significantly, meant that when I sold or refinanced later, I would have a much higher profit margin to work with.

And that's exactly what happened.

I share these stories because I don't want other veterans making the same mistakes I did. The VA Home Loan is one of the most powerful home-buying benefits available, and if you use it wisely, you can avoid the kind of financial chaos I went through.

WHY THE VA HOME LOAN IS YOUR SECRET WEAPON FOR BUILDING WEALTH

If you're a veteran and you're not taking advantage of your VA home loan benefit, you might as well be lighting money on fire. Seriously. The VA home loan is one of the most powerful home-buying tools available, yet so many veterans either never use it or think it's too complicated.

And trust me, I get it. When I first started looking into real estate, I didn't fully understand the power of the VA home loan either. I spent years renting, thinking that homeownership wasn't really in the cards for me at the time. No one sat me down and explained how the VA home loan could be used strategically, not just to buy a home, but to build wealth.

In fact, I personally know far too many veterans who assume they can only use it once, or that it's a one-and-done type of deal. I was almost one of them. But after digging deeper, I realized that not only can you use your VA home loan more than once, but you can also have multiple VA home loans at the same time, meaning you can start building a real estate portfolio while still serving.

The VA home loan is not just a benefit, it's a wealth-building strategy. Used correctly, it can help you:

- **Own property instead of throwing money away on rent**
- **Build equity over time, so you actually get something back for your housing payments**
- **Create rental income by keeping your first home when you PCS and buying another with a VA home loan**
- **Position yourself for financial independence, so you're not just relying on a pension or disability benefits later in life**

Here's a little personal perspective: I've spent years helping fellow veterans navigate real estate, and I can tell you one thing for certain, the people who take advantage of their VA home loan early are in a much better position financially when they leave the military than those who never use it.

I've watched countless veterans regret renting for years when they realize they could've bought a home with zero down, no PMI, and a lower interest rate than conventional loans. Some of them could've had $100,000+ in home equity by the time they transitioned out, but instead, they walked away with nothing. That's a hard lesson to learn.

But it doesn't have to be your story.

Now, before we get into the nitty-gritty, let's address the biggest problem: **VA home loan Myths**. Because trust me, there's a lot of bad information out there, and it's time to set the record straight

BREAKING VA HOME LOAN MYTHS

1. You CAN Use It More Than Once

I can't tell you how many veterans think the VA Home Loan is like a one-and-done deal, like it's a free pass you can only use once in your lifetime. Wrong.

The truth is, you can use your VA Home Loan over and over again as long as you pay off the previous loan or transfer your eligibility by selling the house. Think of it like a reloadable weapon: use it, reset, and use it again. In fact, I know people who have used their VA Home Loan three, four, even five times, upgrading homes or using it strategically to buy investment properties.

Pro Tip: If you sell a home you bought with a VA Home Loan, **you can restore your entitlement and use it again** for another purchase. No need to sit on the sidelines!

2. You CAN Have Multiple VA Home Loans at the Same Time

This one blows people's minds when they find out. Yes, you can actually have more than one VA Home Loan at the same time. Here's how it works: if you still have remaining entitlement, you can use it to buy another home, even while still owning your first VA-financed property.

For example, let's say you're stationed in Virginia, and you buy a home using your VA Home Loan. Then, Uncle Sam decides to send you across the country to San Diego. Instead of selling your home, you rent it out and use your remaining VA Home Loan entitlement to buy another home in San Diego. Boom, now you own two properties!

I've seen people do this and end up with multiple rental properties, all financed using VA Home Loans. If you're smart about it, you can create a real estate portfolio while serving.

Pro Tip: Your entitlement is based on **loan limits per county**. If you're unsure how much you still have left, talk to a VA Home Loan specialist who can break it down for you.

3. There is NO Loan Limit for VA Buyers

I've heard people say, "The VA Home Loan caps how much I can borrow." Not true. The VA used to have loan limits, but they got rid of them in 2020 for VA buyers with full entitlement. That means if you qualify and you have your FULL VA entitlement, you can buy a home for ANY amount as long as the lender approves you.

Now, that doesn't mean you should go buy a mansion just because you can. Let's not go full "E-3 with a Dodge Charger" on this. But it does mean you have more flexibility than most conventional buyers.

Pro Tip: If you've already used your VA Home Loan and haven't restored your full entitlement, you might still have loan limits. But first-time users? Sky's the limit.

4. VA Home Loans Are NOT Harder to Close

Here's a classic one: "Sellers won't accept VA Home Loans because they take too long to close."

While this might have been true twenty years ago, today's VA Home Loan process is just as fast, if not faster, then conventional loans. The average VA Home Loan closes within thirty to forty-five days, which is right in line with other loan types.

So why do sellers still hesitate? Because they don't understand the process. Some real estate agents and sellers think VA buyers have no skin in the game since there's no down payment required. But that's nonsense. The VA backs the loan, making it one of the safest types of financing available.

If a seller pushes back on your VA Home Loan offer, here's how you counter it:

Work with an agent who understands VA Home Loans (hint: not all do)

Have your lender contact the listing agent to explain how smooth the process is

Offer to cover small costs that some sellers fear, like minor repairs or fees

Most of the time, resistance to VA Home Loans is just lack of education. Once sellers understand it, they're usually fine with it.

Pro Tip: If you're in a competitive market, offer slightly above asking price or cover some closing costs to make your VA Home Loan offer more attractive.

5. VA Home Loan Rates Are NOT Higher Than Conventional Loans

This one makes me laugh because the opposite is true: VA Home Loans actually have lower interest rates than conventional loans. Since the government backs VA Home Loans, lenders take on less risk, which means they can offer lower interest rates to veterans.

Here's a quick comparison:

VA Home Loan Interest Rate: Typically, **0.5% to 1% lower** than a conventional loan

Conventional Loan Interest Rate: Higher because there's **more risk for the lender**

Over the course of a 30-year mortgage, a lower interest rate could save you tens of thousands of dollars in interest payments. So next time someone tells you VA Home Loans have higher rates, just smile and say, "Not today, sir."

FINAL THOUGHTS: THE VA HOME LOAN IS A GAME CHANGER–

What I Learned

- Never buy emotionally
- Understand the market and resale risks
- Don't rely solely on others advise - learn the process yourself
- Always plan your exit strategy before you enter the market

Use It Wisely

Use your VA Home Loan more than once – it's a reloadable benefit

Leverage multiple VA Home Loans – you can own more than one home

Don't believe in loan limits – first-time buyers can go as high as they qualify for

VA Home Loans close fast – work with the right lender and agent

Take advantage of lower rates – save thousands in interest

Too many veterans ignore or misunderstand their VA Home Loan benefits, and it costs them big time. This isn't just about buying a home; it's about using your military benefits to create long-term wealth. If you play this right, you won't just be a homeowner, you could be a real estate investor, landlord, and wealth builder before you even leave the military. Don't sleep on this benefit!

I hear and forget. What I write I understand.

NINE
REAL ESTATE AS A WEALTH-BUILDING TOOL

WHY MILITARY FAMILIES SHOULD OWN INSTEAD OF RENT

FOR MANY MILITARY FAMILIES, the idea of homeownership can seem intimidating, especially when frequent PCS moves make it feel like renting is the safer option. I get it; why go through the hassle of buying if you're going to move in a few years, right?

But let me tell you something: every PCS move is a financial opportunity if you approach it the right way. The mistake most military families make is thinking that because they move every few years, they shouldn't buy a home. **Wrong.**

Here's the truth: every PCS move gives you the chance to buy a home, build equity, and create a rental portfolio. The key is understanding how to turn these moves into wealth-building opportunities rather than treating them as temporary disruptions.

THE HIDDEN COST OF RENTING VS. OWNING

Think about all the rent you've paid over the years. If you've been renting for five, ten, or fifteen years, how much money have you spent lining someone else's pockets? Renting is essentially paying someone else's mortgage, while you get nothing in return. You are literally throwing away your BAH every single month with nothing to show for it.

Now imagine if every time you moved, you bought a home instead of renting. Even if you only stayed in that home for three years, you would've been building equity the entire time. Let's break down what equity really means. Equity is the part of your home that you truly own—it's the difference between your home's current market value and the remaining balance on your mortgage.

When you move to your next duty station, instead of walking away with nothing, you could:

- **Sell the home for a profit** (assuming normal appreciation)
- **Rent it out and keep the home as an investment** (turning it into passive income)
- **Leverage your equity for future real estate investments** (using cash-out refinancing or a HELOC)

And here's a huge military-only advantage that makes buying even more profitable: As mentioned before, The **Servicemembers Civil Relief Act (SCRA)** gives active-duty service members a ten-year extension on their capital gains tax exemption for primary residences.

What Does This Mean?

Normally, when a civilian sells their home, they can exclude up to $250,000 in profit from capital gains tax ($500,000 for married couples) if they've lived in the home for at least two of the past five years. But military members get a ten-year extension, meaning that even if you PCS and rent the home out for up to thirteen years after moving, you can still sell it tax-free if you meet the two-year residency requirement. **This is a HUGE advantage that allows military homeowners to sell their properties later and keep more of their profits.**

THE PCS WEALTH-BUILDING STRATEGY

Most civilians don't have the opportunity to relocate every few years with a government-backed zero-down payment loan (VA Home Loan) that they can use repeatedly. Military families do. This means you can strategically acquire properties at multiple duty stations and create a real estate portfolio over your career.

Here's a simple example:

1. **Years One to Three:** A military family buys a home for $250,000 at their first duty station using a VA Home Loan (zero down payment)
2. **Years Four to Six:** After a PCS move, the home appreciates to $280,000. Instead of selling, they keep the home as a rental and want to buy a new home at their next duty station using their VA Home Loan. However, VA entitlement doesn't automatically reset just because they moved. To free up their entitlement, they refinance the original VA loan into a conventional loan, which restores their VA eligibility and allows them to use it again for the next purchase.
3. **Years Seven to Ten:** They continue this process at every duty station, using their BAH to cover mortgage payments instead of paying rent
4. **Years Eleven to Twenty:** By the time they retire, they own three to five rental properties that have appreciated in value and generate steady passive income

Now let's compare two military families after twenty years:

- **The Renting Family:** leaves the military with nothing but memories and zero assets
- **The Buying Family:** leaves the military with a real estate portfolio worth hundreds of thousands (if not millions) of dollars that generates passive income

It's the difference between starting over after retirement versus retiring with financial security.

THE MILITARY REAL ESTATE ADVANTAGE

By leveraging your VA Home Loan and PCS moves wisely, you can set yourself up for financial independence before you even retire from the military. Imagine leaving service with multiple properties generating passive income, providing financial security for you and your family.

This strategy isn't just about buying homes; it's about creating generational wealth. Every duty station is a chance to invest in your future, not just another place to temporarily live.

The Power of Leverage – Owning Appreciating Assets with Little to No Money Down

Leverage is one of the most powerful wealth-building tools in real estate. And guess what? Military members have access to some of the best leverage options available. While most civilians have to save for years to afford a down payment on a home, you have the ability to buy a home with zero down, thanks to the VA Home Loan.

With a VA Home Loan, you can:

- **Buy a home with zero down payment** – This means you can start building wealth without needing tens of thousands of dollars upfront.
- **Avoid private mortgage insurance (PMI)** – PMI is an extra cost that conventional loan borrowers must pay if they put down less than 20%, often adding hundreds of dollars per month to their mortgage payment. With a VA Home Loan, this is **completely waived.**
- **Qualify for lower interest rates** – VA Home Loans typically offer better interest rates than conventional loans, which

means lower monthly payments and more money in your pocket.

Why is this so powerful? Because it allows you to own appreciating assets (real estate) with little to no money out of pocket.

HOW LEVERAGE WORKS IN REAL ESTATE

Let's put this into perspective:

Scenario 1: Buying a Home with a VA Home Loan: Imagine you buy a $300,000 home using a VA Home Loan with $0 down. Now, let's assume your home appreciates by a conservative 3-5% per year.

After five years:

Home value increases to: ~$350,000

Equity gained: $50,000

Initial out-of-pocket investment: $0

That's $50,000 in gained wealth without you doing anything except paying your mortgage and letting the market work in your favor.

Scenario 2: Renting Instead of Buying: Now, let's say you choose to rent instead because you're worried about moving in a few years. You're paying $2,500 per month in rent (a common rate near many military bases).

After five years:

Total rent paid: $150,000

Homeownership benefits gained: ZERO

Equity built: NONE

That's $150,000 gone forever. You paid someone else's mortgage, and at the end of five years, you walk away with nothing to show for it.

. . .

Scenario 3: Buying and Holding for Long-Term Wealth: Now, let's say instead of selling your home when you PCS, you keep it as a rental property and let someone else pay your mortgage.

After five years, your home is worth $350,000, and instead of selling, you rent it out for $2,500 per month (the same amount you would have paid in rent).

Your **tenant pays your mortgage**

Your **home continues appreciating**

You **generate passive income**

This is what wealthy people understand: real estate builds wealth over time, and the earlier you start, the more you gain. The military gives you a unique advantage with the VA Home Loan to own appreciating assets without upfront costs, and if you take advantage of it early in your career, you can set yourself up for financial independence before you even leave the service.

Why Most People Don't Leverage This Opportunity

The biggest mistake military members make? Thinking they need to wait until after they separate to start investing in real estate.

COMMON EXCUSES & WHY THEY'RE WRONG

"I don't want to deal with managing a rental property."

Solution: Hire a property manager. They take 7-10% of the monthly rent and handle everything: tenant screening, repairs, rent collection, and more.

"I might not make money right away."

Solution: Even if you break even on rent vs. mortgage, your tenants are still paying off your loan for you. That means in fifteen to thirty years, you own the home free and clear, and everything it's worth is yours.

"I'm worried about selling when I PCS."

Solution: Thanks to the SCRA, you have up to thirteen years after moving to sell your home tax-free and exclude up to $500,000 in capital gains. This means you can wait for the market to go up before selling when you PCS.

The Choice is Yours

At the end of the day, you're going to pay to live somewhere. The only question is: do you want to pay for someone else's mortgage or your own? The VA Home Loan is one of the most powerful wealth-building tools available, and it's exclusively for service members, veterans, and their families. If you take advantage of it early in your military career, you set yourself up for financial success long after you leave the service.

So, the next time you PCS, don't just look for a place to rent, look for an investment opportunity.

TURNING YOUR HOME INTO AN INVESTMENT

If you're planning to buy a home at your next duty station, think like an investor. Too many service members treat buying a home like picking an apartment; it's all about what looks nice and feels comfortable in the moment. But if you shift your mindset from ***home-buyer*** to ***real estate investor***, every home purchase can become a long-term wealth-building asset.

Instead of just asking ***"Where do I want to live,"*** ask yourself:

- **Will this home appreciate in value?** Are property values in this area trending upward? Is there economic growth nearby (new businesses, schools, infrastructure)?
- **Can I rent this out for a profit when I move?** Does the local rental market support strong rental income? Will your mortgage be covered (or even exceeded) by rent?

- **Is this home in a good location with strong demand?** Is it near a military base, major employer, or a desirable school district, ensuring long-term rental potential?
- **Does this home fit within my budget and financial goals?** Can you afford this home without stretching your finances too thin? Does it allow room for future investments?

By being strategic about where and what you buy, every PCS move can turn into a long-term financial opportunity.

HOW TO TURN YOUR HOME INTO A MONEY-MAKING ASSET

Buy a property in a growing area. Housing markets in strong job hubs appreciate faster and attract good renters. Look for areas with consistent population and job growth, ensuring demand remains high when you decide to rent or sell.

Use your VA Home Loan to minimize upfront costs. Since you can buy with zero down, you keep more cash in reserves for future investments. Many real estate investors start with a single home and scale up by leveraging profits and equity from their first property.

Rent out the home when you PCS. Military bases always have a demand for rentals because service members are moving in and out constantly. Even if you only break even at first, your tenant is paying your mortgage for you, which means you're building wealth for free.

Leverage equity to buy more properties. As your home appreciates, you can refinance or pull equity to buy more real estate. Many investors use cash-out refinances or HELOCs (Home Equity Lines of Credit) to fund additional property purchases without using their own cash.

Know the SCRA Benefits. Remember, active-duty service members get a ten-year capital gains tax exemption extension under SCRA. This means that instead of the normal three-year exemption window, you now have thirteen years to sell your home and claim between

$250,000 to $500,000 (depending if you are married or not) in tax-free profits! This is a HUGE advantage that most civilians don't get, take advantage of it!

Final Thoughts: Real Estate is Your Fastest Path to Wealth

Stop renting and start owning. Every PCS move is a chance to build equity instead of throwing money away.

Leverage VA Home Loans to buy homes with zero down. You don't need to be rich to start investing in real estate: your military benefits already put you ahead of the game.

Turn every home purchase into a long-term investment. Even if you move, your home can become a cash-flowing rental, creating passive income for you.

Real estate appreciates over time. What seems expensive now will likely be worth much more in ten to twenty years.

The bottom line? If you're serious about financial security, start looking at real estate as an investment, not just a place to live. Use every PCS move as an opportunity to build your real estate portfolio, so when you leave the military, you've already built wealth.

I hear and forget. What I write I understand.

TEN
REAL ESTATE INVESTMENT STRATEGIES

TURNING REAL ESTATE INTO A MONEY-MAKING MACHINE

BY NOW, you understand that owning real estate is one of the fastest ways to build wealth—but let's take it a step further. Owning a home is great, but investing in real estate strategically is what truly sets you up for financial independence.

A lot of people think you need to be rich to be a real estate investor. Nope! You just need to be smart. And the best part? As a service member or veteran, you have built-in advantages that make investing easier than it is for the average civilian.

VA Home Loan = No Down Payment – While civilians need to save up thousands for a down payment, you can buy real estate with zero money out of pocket.

PCS-Proofing Your Investment – Every PCS move is a real estate opportunity, if you buy wisely, you can turn each home into a rental when you move.

Tax Benefits & Capital Gains Exemptions – Don't forget that SCRA Tax exemption mentioned earlier.

LESSONS LEARNED THE HARD WAY

Let me tell you a little story about how I did everything wrong before I learned to do it right.

Lesson #1 – The Nightmare Rental Property

Remember the tenant who cost me $250,000? I already walked you through that disaster back in Chapter 4, but it's worth revisiting here —because that experience didn't just damage a property, it completely changed how I approach real estate as a business.

Back then, I thought I had everything figured out. I bought a rental property and assumed all I had to do was hand over the keys and wait for the rent checks to roll in. What I failed to do was properly screen the tenant. That one oversight brought me face-to-face with someone who knew exactly how to manipulate the system.

She paid exactly one month's rent and then stopped completely. But instead of avoiding the situation, she leaned into it. She knew the law inside and out—better than I did, and better than my own real estate agent. She used every trick in the book to delay the eviction process, filing extensions, making last-minute legal claims, and dragging the entire process out for nine long months.

For nine months, she lived in that home rent-free. And when I finally got the legal clearance to remove her, the damage was done—literally. The house was destroyed. There were holes in the walls, broken appliances, carpet stains that couldn't be explained, and an overall level of damage that made it look like a demolition crew had lived there.

That was the moment I realized that real estate isn't just about buying property—it's about managing risk. And it starts with who you allow through the front door.

The lesson? Screen your tenants like you're hiring for the Secret Service. Verify everything—employment, income, credit, criminal history, and rental references. Don't accept excuses or skip steps because someone "seems nice" or "just needs a break."

If they lead with a sob story, take it seriously—but not emotionally. This isn't about heart. It's about smart. Real estate is a business. And if you don't treat it like one, you will pay the price. I did.

Lesson #2 – Don't Get Emotionally Attached

When I bought my first home, I thought it was just that, a home. I didn't think of it as an investment. Big mistake. I made choices based on what I liked, rather than what would make the most financial sense.

For example, instead of buying a property in a high-demand rental area, I bought a house because I liked the backyard. Spoiler alert: backyards don't pay mortgages, tenants do.

Fast forward a few years, and I struggled to rent the home because it wasn't in a prime rental location. If I had thought like an investor instead of a homeowner, I would have bought in a hot rental market where my property would be in demand long after I moved.

Lesson learned? Buy with your calculator, not your heart.

HOW TO MAKE YOUR REAL ESTATE WORK FOR YOU

Now that you know what not to do, let's talk about how to make your real estate work for you like a well-oiled money machine.

Buy Properties in High-Demand Areas – If your property is near a military base, hospital, or major employer, you'll always have a steady stream of potential renters.

Set Rent to Cover (or Exceed) Your Mortgage – The goal is to have someone else pay off your investment for you while you build equity.

Leverage Your Equity – As your home appreciates, use that equity to buy additional properties and grow your real estate portfolio.

Screen Tenants Like Your Life Depends on It – Trust me, one bad tenant can cost you thousands. Run background checks, call previous landlords, and never rent to anyone who "just needs a break."

Treat It Like a Business – Your property is not just a home: it's a long-term asset that should generate income. Make decisions based on numbers, not emotions.

REAL ESTATE IS YOUR FINANCIAL FREEDOM VEHICLE

The military gives you a huge advantage when it comes to real estate investing, but only if you use it. Too many service members waste their VA Home Loan on a single home and never invest again. But if you use every PCS move as an opportunity, you can retire from the military with a real estate portfolio that generates passive income for life.

So, here's my challenge to you: **Stop thinking of real estate as just a place to live. Start thinking of it as the key to financial freedom.** Invest wisely, leverage your VA benefits, and turn every home into a wealth-building asset.

SHORT-TERM VS. MID-TERM VS. LONG-TERM RENTALS – MAXIMIZING YOUR RENTAL STRATEGY

If you own a home, you've got more than just two options when it comes to making money from it. Instead of choosing just between short-term (Airbnb) or long-term (traditional twelve-month lease) rentals, there's also a powerful middle ground: Mid-Term Rentals (MTRs).

So, what are your three main rental strategies?

1. **Short-Term Rentals (STRs)** – Think Airbnb, VRBO, and vacation rentals

2. **Mid-Term Rentals (MTRs)** – Fully furnished rentals for thirty plus days, catering to traveling professionals, military families, and digital nomads
3. **Long-Term Rentals (LTRs)** – Traditional twelve-month leases with steady tenants

Each comes with its own advantages and challenges but having a property that can pivot between STRs and MTRs can be a total game-changer.

SHORT-TERM RENTALS – HIGH RISK, HIGH REWARD

The idea of running an Airbnb sounds amazing: charge people $200 a night instead of $2,000 a month? Count me in! But before you start picturing yourself as a luxury Airbnb mogul, let me tell you, it's not all easy money.

I once stayed in an Airbnb that looked perfect online: gorgeous photos, a stocked kitchen, and even a cute little welcome basket. But the moment I walked in, I realized those photos were clearly taken in 2014 because this place had seen some things since then. The fridge was broken, the bed squeaked louder than a Navy Chief's knees, and I swear something was living in the walls. That's when I realized that hosting short-term rentals is a full-time job. Guests can be amazing, or they can be the reason you lose sleep.

Pros of STRs:

Higher income potential – you can make two to three times more than a long-term rental

Flexibility – block off dates and use the property yourself

Military-friendly – if you PCS, you can Airbnb instead of selling

Cons of STRs:

Lots of maintenance & cleaning – you're turning over guests constantly

Uncertain income – some months might be fully booked, others dead quiet

City regulations – many areas ban short-term rentals or heavily tax them

MID-TERM RENTALS – THE HIDDEN GEM FOR MILITARY LANDLORDS

MTRs are the secret weapon that most investors overlook. These are fully furnished rentals for stays of thirty days or more, catering to:

Traveling nurses (high demand year-round)

Remote workers & digital nomads who want a flexible living situation

Military families needing temporary housing during a PCS transition

Corporate renters who need short-term housing for employees

The **real advantage? Less turnover than STRs, but higher profit than LTRs.**

Pros of MTRs:

Less turnover than Airbnb – no weekly guests to manage

Higher rent than traditional leases – you can charge 30-50% more than a standard rental

Fewer city regulations – Most STR laws don't apply to thirty plus day stays.

Military PCS-proof – Perfect for short-term military housing.

Cons of MTRs:

Smaller tenant pool – you're relying on a niche market (but it's growing fast)

Furnishing required – you need to provide a fully furnished space

More management than LTRs – tenants rotate every few months, so you need a system in place

Why this works for military landlords: if you PCS, you can list your home as a mid-term rental for other incoming service members instead of selling it. Many families need temporary housing for two to six months while waiting for base housing or closing on a new home. And if you have a break between mid-term renters, you can shift the property to a STR until you get another mid-term renter.

LONG-TERM RENTALS – THE SET-IT-AND-FORGET-IT APPROACH

On the flip side, **long-term rentals (LTRs)** are way easier. You find a good tenant, set up a twelve-month lease, and let the rent checks roll in.

Pros of LTRs:

Consistent, stable income – you know exactly what you're making each month

Less turnover – no need to constantly find new renters

Lower costs – no daily or weekly cleaning fees

Cons of LTRs:

Tenant issues – a bad tenant can be a nightmare and cost you thousands

Less flexibility – harder to use the property for yourself

Missed profit potential – you might be leaving money on the table compared to STRs or MTRs

The Best Strategy? A Rental That Can Pivot

The real magic happens when you buy a home that can switch between STRs, MTRs, and LTRs. If short-term rental regulations change in your city, you can switch to mid-term rentals and still keep your property profitable.

Example: A Military Landlord Strategy

You buy a home near a base and live in it while stationed there

When you PCS, you convert it into a mid-term rental for military families

If demand shifts, you list it as a long-term rental for steady cash flow

You leverage your equity to buy another home at your next duty station

This flexibility protects your investment and ensures that your real estate continues making you money, whether you're living in it or not.

MAXIMIZE YOUR RENTAL INCOME

Short-Term Rentals: High profit, high maintenance, high risk. Best for those who can actively manage the property or hire a property manager.

Mid-Term Rentals: Lower maintenance, great income, stable demand. Ideal for military landlords, travel nurses, and corporate renters.

Long-Term Rentals: Hands-off, steady income, long-term wealth building. Best for those who want passive income with minimal management.

The key takeaway? A furnished property that can pivot between STRs, MTRs, and LTRs is the ultimate rental strategy. It future-proofs your investment, keeps you adaptable, and maximizes your returns. So, if you're planning to buy a home, think beyond just where you'll live. Think about how you can turn it into a money-making machine, long after you PCS.

HOUSE HACKING & MULTI-UNIT INVESTMENTS – LIVING FOR FREE WHILE RENTING OUT PORTIONS OF YOUR HOME

House hacking is hands-down one of the best-kept secrets in real estate investing, especially for military service members and veterans. Why? Because you can use your VA Home Loan (zero down!) to buy multi-unit properties, making it possible to live for free while your tenants cover the mortgage.

This is a real-life cheat code for building wealth, and I wish I had started this way. Instead of just buying a home to live in, I could've been making money from day one while still having a place to live.

How House Hacking Works:

Step 1: Buy a duplex, triplex, or fourplex using your VA Home Loan (zero down payment required).

Step 2: Live in one unit and rent out the others.

Step 3: Use your tenants' rent payments to cover your mortgage, taxes, and insurance.

Step 4: Enjoy living for free (or close to it) while building equity and cash flow. Example of a Military House Hack:

- You buy a quadplex for $500,000 near a military base
- Your mortgage (including taxes & insurance) is $3,000/month
- You live in one unit and rent out the other three for $1,200 each ($3,600 total)
- Now, your tenants are paying your entire mortgage, and you have extra cash flow every month

Sounds too good to be true? It's not. It's just a smart financial move that too many service members overlook.

Don't Have a Multi-Unit Property? You Can Still House Hack!

Even if you only buy a single-family home, you can still house hack by renting out extra rooms.

Military House Hacking Option:

- Buy a three or four-bedroom home near base using your VA Home Loan (zero down)
- Rent out the extra bedrooms to other service members
- Charge them BAH-friendly rates that still undercut the local rental market
- Live for free or dramatically reduce your housing costs

Example:

- You buy a four-bedroom home near base, with a $2,500/month mortgage
- You rent out three rooms to fellow service members for $800 each ($2,400 total)
- Your out-of-pocket cost to live there? Just $100/month

Imagine how much extra money you'd have to invest, pay off debt, or save for another property.

Why House Hacking is the Ultimate Military Investment Strategy:

You build wealth instead of throwing money away on rent

Your housing costs drop significantly—or disappear completely

You get experience as a landlord while still having the safety of a full-time income

You can transition your property into a long-term rental or mid-term rental when you PCS

What I Wish I Had Known Sooner

Looking back, I kicked myself for not house hacking from the start. I could've been setting myself up financially years earlier. But here's the good news: it's never too late to start. Whether you're just getting into real estate or already own a home, you can use this strategy to dramatically change your financial future. If you're still renting or thinking about buying a home, don't just buy to live, buy to invest. House hacking can be your launch pad to financial freedom.

REAL ESTATE HACKS FOR SERVICE MEMBERS – PROTECTING & GROWING YOUR INVESTMENTS

As a military member, you have real estate advantages that most civilians could only dream of. You can buy homes with zero down, access government-backed loans, and move frequently, all of which can be turned into wealth-building opportunities when done strategically. But there's one key element many service members overlook: protecting their investments.

When you start building a real estate portfolio, you need to think beyond just buying homes, you need to protect your assets for the long haul. That's where LLCs and trusts come in. But before we dive into that, let's cover the foundational real estate hacks that set you up for financial success.

1. Renting Rooms to Fellow Service Members

If you're single and own a home, you have an easy way to make extra money—renting rooms to other service members. Think about it: every military base is filled with young service members looking for affordable, off-base housing. Instead of letting them pay rent to a stranger, why not make that rental income yourself?

Example: I knew a guy, let's call him *"Smart Sergeant Steve."* Steve bought a four-bedroom home near base using his VA Home Loan (zero down). He lived in one bedroom and rented out the other three to fellow E-5s for $800 per room.

His mortgage payment? $2,400 per month

His rental income? $2,400 per month

His total cost of living? ZERO

Instead of paying rent every month, Steve was living for free while building home equity. And when he PCSed, he converted the home into a long-term rental, keeping it as an investment.

The Takeaway:

- Buy a larger home than you need
- Rent out the extra rooms to fellow service members
- Let them cover your mortgage while you build wealth

It's house hacking at its finest!

2. Using VA Home Loans for Multi-Unit Properties

Most people think the VA Home Loan is just for single-family homes, but that's completely false. Did you know you can use your VA Home Loan to buy a two-unit, three-unit, or even a four-unit property with ZERO down? That means you can live in one unit and rent out the rest, allowing your tenants to pay your mortgage while you build wealth.

Example: I once met an officer who used his VA Home Loan to buy a fourplex near a military base.

- He lived in one unit and rented out the other three
- His tenants covered his entire mortgage payment
- By the time he PCSd, he had a cash-flowing investment property that was paying him every month

The Best Part?

- You don't need a huge down payment (VA Home Loan = $0 down)
- You get a lower interest rate compared to conventional loans
- Your rental income builds equity while you live for free

Pro Tip: If you're single or newly married, buy a multi-unit property early in your career so that by the time you separate from the military, you'll already have passive rental income.

3. PCS-Proofing Your Investment Strategy

PCS moves are part of military life, but instead of letting them ruin your finances, you can turn them into real estate opportunities. The biggest mistake military members make? Selling their home every time they move. Instead of selling, keep your homes as rental properties and build a real estate portfolio.

Buy in areas with strong rental demand

- Military bases always have incoming service members looking for housing
- Look for properties near base or in high-demand rental areas

Make sure your mortgage payment is covered by rent

- Before buying, run the numbers
- Check Zillow, Apartments.com, or Facebook Marketplace to see how much similar homes rent for
- If your future rent can cover your mortgage, it's a solid investment

Be flexible—short-term, mid-term, or long-term rentals

- **Long-Term Rentals (twelve-month leases)** are stable but require the right tenants

- **Mid-Term Rentals (three to six months, furnished)** are perfect for traveling nurses, military families, and corporate professionals
- **Short-Term Rentals (Airbnb/VRBO)** can be highly profitable, but some cities regulate them heavily

Pro Tip: If you furnish your home, you can pivot between long-term, mid-term, or short-term rentals based on demand. This way, your property remains profitable even if rental market conditions change.

Hire a property manager to handle everything while you're stationed elsewhere.

- If you don't want to deal with tenants while you're deployed or stationed overseas, hire a property manager (they typically take 8-12% of the rent)
- This allows you to own rental properties anywhere without having to worry about maintenance or tenants calling you at 2AM

4. Protecting Your Investments with LLCs and Trusts

As you start building your real estate portfolio, protecting your assets becomes just as important as acquiring them.

Why You Need an LLC for Rental Properties

An LLC (Limited Liability Company) separates your personal finances from your rental properties. If a tenant sues you, your personal assets (like your savings, house, and car) are protected.

Protects **your personal assets from lawsuits**

Allows **you to keep rental income separate from personal finances**

May **offer tax benefits depending on how it's structured**

Pro Tip: If you own multiple properties, consider setting up separate LLCs for each one to further shield your assets.

Why You Should Consider a Trust

If you own multiple properties or want to pass real estate to your heirs without dealing with probate, setting up a real estate trust is a smart move.

Avoids **probate when passing properties to family members**

Provides **privacy—your properties won't be publicly tied to your name**

Offers **estate planning benefits and asset protection**

Pro Tip: Many high-net-worth individuals place their real estate into trusts to protect assets from lawsuits, taxes, and probate delays. As you grow your portfolio, this is something to consider.

MAKE MILITARY MOVES WORK FOR YOU

Military life means moving frequently, so turn every move into a real estate opportunity

- Rent out extra rooms to service members and let them cover your mortgage
- Use your VA Home Loan to buy multi-unit properties and build rental income
- PCS-proof your real estate strategy by keeping properties as rentals instead of selling them
- Set up LLCs and trusts to protect your real estate investments

If you take advantage of these real estate hacks, you'll have a passive income portfolio before you even separate from the military. Start thinking like an investor now, and your future self will thank you.

Tax Benefits of Real Estate for Military Investors – Keep More of Your Money

One of the biggest advantages of investing in real estate isn't just the rental income or appreciation, it's the tax benefits. And as a service member or veteran, you get even more perks than the average investor.

The tax code is written to incentivize property ownership because the government wants people to invest in housing. If you understand how to use these benefits to your advantage, you'll keep more of your hard-earned money instead of handing it over to the IRS.

Let's break down the key tax benefits that military real estate investors can use to build wealth faster.

Mortgage Interest Deduction – Pay Less in Taxes

For many homeowners, mortgage interest is one of the biggest expenses. But the good news? It's tax-deductible.

Deduct **the interest you pay on your mortgage each year**

Applies **to both primary residences and rental properties**

Lowers **your taxable income, which reduces the amount you owe in taxes**

Example: If you paid $10,000 in mortgage interest this year and your taxable income was $80,000, you now only pay taxes on $70,000 instead of $80,000. That's a huge savings!

Depreciation – The IRS Lets You Write Off Property Value Over Time

Real estate depreciation is one of the best-kept secrets in tax law. The IRS lets property owners deduct a portion of their property's value each year because homes "wear out" over time (even though they usually increase in value!).

Deduct a portion of your property's value from your taxable income every year

This is a paper loss, you're not actually losing money, but the IRS treats it as if you are

Even if your rental property is cash-flow positive, depreciation can reduce or eliminate taxes on your rental income

Example: If you own a $300,000 rental property, the IRS lets you depreciate the home over twenty-seven and a half years. This means you can deduct about $10,900 per year in depreciation, even though your home is likely increasing in value!

Pro Tip: Many military investors combine depreciation with other deductions to pay little or no taxes on their rental income.

Capital Gains Exclusion – Tax-Free Home Sales for Military Members

One of the biggest tax advantages of owning real estate is the ability to sell your home tax-free and keep the profits. Normally, when you sell an investment that has gone up in value, you owe capital gains tax. But if you live in your home for at least two out of the last five years, you can sell it tax-free up to:

$250,000 if you're single

$500,000 if you're married

Example: Let's say you bought a home for $300,000 and sold it five years later for $450,000. That's $150,000 in profit. If you qualify for the capital gains exclusion, you owe $0 in taxes on that money.

Military Bonus: The PCS Exemption

PCS Exemption – Extra Capital Gains Flexibility for Service Members

I know I mentioned this a couple of times before but that's how important this benefit is to build wealth while on active duty. For most civilians, you must live in a home for two of the last five years to sell it tax-free. But military members get a special exemption thanks to the SCRA.

If **you receive PCS orders, the IRS extends your capital gains exclusion by an additional ten years!**

That **means you could own a home for up to fifteen years, rent it out for most of that time, and still sell it tax-free!**

Example:

- You buy a home in San Diego in 2010 while stationed at Naval Base Coronado
- You lived in it for two years, then received PCS orders in 2012 and rented it out
- In 2025, you decide to sell the home for a $300,000 profit
- Because of the PCS exemption, you still qualify for the tax-free sale, despite not living there since 2012

This huge benefit allows military homeowners to build wealth through appreciation without worrying about tax penalties.

Bonus: Deduct Rental Property Expenses

If you own rental properties, the IRS allows you to deduct many of your expenses related to managing and maintaining them.

Property **management fees**

Repairs **& maintenance**

Landlord **insurance**

Property **taxes**

Advertising **for tenants**

Utilities **(if you pay them)**

Pro Tip: Keep detailed records of all expenses related to your rental properties so you can maximize deductions come tax time.

Keep More of Your Hard-Earned Money

The tax code rewards real estate investors, especially military service members and veterans.

Maximize your tax benefits by:

Deducting mortgage interest and depreciation to lower taxable income

Using the capital gains exclusion to sell homes tax-free

Leveraging the PCS exemption for even greater flexibility

Writing off rental property expenses to reduce your tax bill

If you use these strategies smartly, real estate can not only generate income but also save you thousands in taxes every year. Understanding these benefits is the key to building long-term financial security.

FINAL THOUGHTS: REAL ESTATE IS THE MILITARY'S BEST KEPT SECRET

Use VA Home Loans to buy income-generating properties

House hack to reduce or eliminate your mortgage

Take advantage of short-term or long-term rentals

PCS-proof your investments to keep properties for the long haul

By using these strategies, you can turn military benefits into real estate wealth.

I hear and forget. What I write I understand.

ELEVEN
TRANSITIONING FROM MILITARY TO CIVILIAN LIFE FINANCIALLY STRONG

THE REALITY OF TRANSITIONING: FROM PAYCHECKS TO PANIC

AS I TOUCHED ON EARLIER, the end of your military paycheck is more than just a financial shock—it's a psychological one. But this chapter is about preparing for that shift with confidence. Transitioning from military to civilian life is a wild ride, and no matter how prepared you think you are, there's always that moment of panic. One day, you have a steady paycheck, free healthcare, and a structured mission, and the next day, you're staring at your DD-214 like it's a puzzle missing half the pieces, thinking, "What the hell do I do now?"

I've been there. When I left the Navy, I thought I had everything figured out, real estate was my new mission, but even then, the transition was a shock. Suddenly, I was responsible for everything, no more guaranteed paycheck on the 1st and 15th, no more automatic promotions, and definitely no more free healthcare.

And let's be real, when you transition out, you're not just leaving a job; you're leaving behind an entire way of life. In the military, we had a clear structure, a chain of command, and a predictable career progression. Civilian life? Not so much. Promotions aren't automatic, job security isn't guaranteed, and your value in the workforce is based on performance, not time in service.

Here's where the financial gut check happens:

- **That steady BAH? Gone.**
- **That built-in life insurance? You have to find your own.**
- **Those tax-free benefits? Yeah, kiss those goodbye.**
- **That guaranteed retirement check (if you didn't stay for twenty years)? Hope you saved, because now you're on your own.**

WHY SO MANY VETERANS STRUGGLE FINANCIALLY AFTER TRANSITION

Here's the hard truth: many veterans struggle financially because they don't plan ahead. The paycheck stops, but the bills keep coming. The average transition timeline is about six to twelve months before landing a solid civilian job, but many don't have enough savings to cover that gap.

Some fall into the "I'll figure it out later" trap, only to realize that later comes fast and hits hard. Others underestimate how difficult it can be to translate military skills into civilian job opportunities, leaving them underemployed or unemployed longer than expected.

And let's not forget about the financial booby traps waiting for veterans:

- **Cashing out the TSP** – Many separating service members cash out their TSP without realizing the massive tax penalties that come with it.
- **Living like you still have BAH** – Some veterans keep spending like they're still getting tax-free housing allowances, only to realize their civilian paycheck doesn't stretch as far.
- **Ignoring VA Benefits** – Many don't take advantage of VA

programs that could ease the financial burden, from VA healthcare to home loans.

HOW TO TRANSITION WITHOUT GOING BROKE

The key to transitioning financially strong is to start planning while you're still in uniform. If you wait until you're already out, you're playing catch-up, and trust me, that's not a game you want to play.

Here's what you should **start doing NOW** before you separate:

- **Build an emergency fund.** Have at least **6 months of living expenses saved up** before your last paycheck hits.
- **Develop a post-military budget.** Your income will change, your expenses will change: plan for it.
- **Tap into SkillBridge or Apprenticeship Programs.** These programs let you train for a new career while still getting paid by the military.
- **Get your VA Benefits squared away.** File for disability compensation, enroll in VA healthcare, and understand your educational benefits.
- **Lock in life insurance. SGLI ends 120 days after separation,** and if you wait too long, private insurance could be way more expensive. You can convert your SGLI to Veterans Group Life Insurance(VGLI) or another policy if desired.
- **Learn how to maximize your civilian income.** Whether that's real estate, starting a business, or investing, you need multiple streams of income.

The bottom line? **Your last day in uniform is NOT the time to start figuring this out.** Start planning today so that when you separate, you're financially prepared, not financially panicked.

SkillBridge & Apprenticeship Programs – The Two-Phase Transition to a Real Estate and other career paths

One of the best-kept secrets for transitioning service members is the **SkillBridge Program,** a DOD-approved internship that allows active-duty personnel to work with a civilian company for up to six months before they separate, all while still receiving full military pay and benefits. Here is just one path to consider using these programs. At Military Operated Real Estate (MORE), we've taken this one step further.

We've developed a **two-phase transition process** that **no** other real estate company in the country offers, leveraging both SkillBridge and the VA-approved Apprenticeship Program to provide a fully supported path into real estate while making sure service members still get paid during training.

Phase 1: SkillBridge – Get Paid While Interning with MORE

Intern in real estate while still on active duty

Learn the fundamentals of real estate sales, contracts, and negotiations

Work alongside top-producing agents and start building your network

Our SkillBridge partnership allows service members to start their real estate journey before they even separate. During this phase, interns gain hands-on experience, attend training, and learn how to run a real estate business, all while still getting paid by the military. The goal of Phase 1 is to help you get your real estate license before separation, so when you leave active duty, you already have a clear career path and an income strategy.

Phase 2: The MORE Apprenticeship Program – The Only VA-Approved Real Estate Apprenticeship in the U.S.

Once you earn your real estate license, you can transition into our exclusive VA-approved Apprenticeship Program, the only one in the country approved by the Department of Veterans Affairs. At this stage, you can now use your VA education benefits to receive a monthly housing stipend while building your real estate business.

What Makes This So Powerful?

You get paid while learning – Unlike most real estate agents who struggle financially in their first year, our apprentices receive a VA housing stipend while training.

Structured mentorship & coaching – Learn from top-producing military-affiliated real estate professionals.

Build your business the right way – We don't just teach you how to sell homes; we teach you how to build a sustainable real estate career with proven systems.

Use VA benefits without going to college – Many veterans assume their education benefits only apply to traditional schooling. We've broken that mold by creating a hands-on, income-generating pathway into real estate.

WHY THIS MATTERS FOR YOUR TRANSITION

Most veterans leave the military with no clear financial plan. They scramble to find jobs, often taking pay cuts and struggling with the transition. With SkillBridge plus the MORE Apprenticeship Program, we've created a seamless, financially supported transition into real estate, helping service members go from active duty to successful business owners without experiencing the financial instability that plagues so many veterans after separation.

No one else is doing this. Start while you're on active duty. Get licensed. Get paid during training. Build a business. Secure your financial future. If you're serious about making real estate your next mission, let's get you on the right path, while making sure you still get paid every step of the way. It's not just about real estate, it's about learning business, leadership, and financial independence. If you're getting out of the military, you need to find an industry that pays well, offers flexibility, and doesn't cap your potential, and real estate is one of those industries.

But real estate isn't for everyone, and that's fine, there are SkillBridge programs for nearly every industry, from cybersecurity to project management to skilled trades. The important thing is that you start looking into these opportunities at least a year before you separate.

Pro Tip: Many companies that offer SkillBridge end up hiring their interns full-time, meaning you can have a civilian job lined up before you even leave the military.

STARTING A VETERAN-OWNED BUSINESS - SBA LOANS, GRANTS, AND RESOURCES

Entrepreneurship is another great path for veterans, and trust me, I've been on both sides of it. From my real estate businesses like The Winfield Group to my nonprofit work with the Enlisted Leadership Foundation, and even my failed brewery business, Inland Wharf Brewing Company (more on that later), I've seen the highs and lows of running a business.

SBA LOAN OPTIONS FOR VETERANS

Veteran entrepreneurs have several **Small Business Administration (SBA)** loan programs designed to make financing more accessible. These loans often come with reduced fees or better terms for veterans, provided the business is at least 51% veteran-owned

Key loan options include:

- **SBA 7(a) Veterans Advantage** – The flagship SBA 7(a) loan program offers up to $5 million for small businesses, and veterans benefit from fee waivers on smaller loans. SBA's Veterans Advantage initiative waives the upfront guaranty fee (typically 2–3%) on 7(a) loans up to $150,000. For larger loans, qualified veteran-owned businesses get a 50% reduction in guaranty fees. This can save thousands in loan costs, making it easier to start or expand a business. Eligibility requires majority (51%+) ownership by an honorably discharged veteran, service-disabled veteran, active Guard/Reserve member, or spouse/widow of a veteran. The 7(a) funds can be used for working capital, equipment, franchise purchases, or refinancing debt, with long repayment terms (seven to ten years for working capital, up to twenty-five years for real estate).

SBA Express Loans – A subset of 7(a), SBA Express is known for faster turnaround (often within thirty-six hours) and lower loan amounts (capped at $500,000). For veterans, the SBA Express program *waives all upfront guaranty fees on loans up to $350,000*, significantly reducing out-of-pocket costs. These loans still require good credit (often ~650+ FICO) and some business track record, but they provide quicker access to funding for immediate needs. The trade-off is they generally have slightly higher interest rates and shorter terms than standard 7(a) loans.

- **Military Reservist Economic Injury Disaster Loan (MREIDL)** – This is a special SBA disaster loan program for businesses whose owner or essential employee is called to active duty in the National Guard or Reserve. If your business suffers economic injury because a key employee deploys, MREIDL can provide low-interest loans to cover operating expenses until the employee returns. It's not for startup capital, but rather a safety net to keep the business running during a deployment-related hardship. MREIDL loans can help veteran-owned companies avoid bankruptcy or severe losses when duty calls.
- **SBA Microloans and Community Advantage** – For veterans launching newer ventures or needing smaller amounts, the SBA microloan program offers loans up to $50,000, often

through nonprofit lenders. These microloans have higher interest (typically 6–9%) but more flexible credit requirements, helping early-stage businesses get funding for inventory, equipment, or working capital. Similarly, the **Community Advantage** program under 7(a) targets underserved borrowers including veterans, with loans up to $350,000 and an SBA guaranty of up to 85%. Community Advantage lenders (like certified nonprofits and community lenders) may be more willing to lend to a startup or a vet with a modest credit profile.

While veterans can of course apply for standard **SBA 504 loans** (for real estate/equipment) or other SBA financing, the above programs are most tailored to veterans' needs. Always prepare a solid business plan and documentation of your veteran status (e.g. DD214 form) when applying, and leverage your local SBA office or **Veterans Business Outreach Center** for guidance on the application process.

VETERAN-SPECIFIC GRANTS

Unlike loans, grants provide funding that does not need to be repaid, essentially free money for your business. While business grants are highly competitive and less common than loans, there are several veteran-focused grants and competitions worth pursuing. Each has its own eligibility criteria and application process. Here are a few notable ones for veteran entrepreneurs:

- **Second Service Foundation's Military Entrepreneur Challenge** – The Second Service Foundation (formerly the StreetShares Foundation) runs a pitch competition where veterans and military spouses can win business grant money. To apply, you must register online and attend a required speed coaching session. Applicants then submit an application package including a one-page business overview. If selected as a finalist, you'll deliver a live pitch at a foundation event for a chance at cash grants (the top prize varies by event). This program is a great way to sharpen your business plan and potentially win **non-dilutive funding**. Past winners have received anywhere from a few thousand dollars up to $15,000 or more to fuel their businesses.

- **Warrior Rising Startup Grants – Warrior Rising** is a nonprofit that transforms veterans into "vetrepreneurs" through a multi-step business development program. They offer training, coaching, mentoring, and networking as part of their process. Veterans (or immediate family members) who complete the program gain the opportunity to pitch their business idea and compete for startup grant funding. Both startups and existing businesses can apply to Warrior Rising; an application and proof of veteran status are required. Notably, in 2023 Warrior Rising's annual **Business Shower** event awarded a record $300,000 in grants to veteran-owned startups, including a **$150,000 grant to the first-place business** (a veteran couple's property management startup). This illustrates the scale of funding available through such competitions, along with the training and mentorship that come with it.
- **Hiring Our Heroes Small Business Grants** – The U.S. Chamber of Commerce Foundation's Hiring Our Heroes initiative offers an annual Small Business Award for Veterans and Military Spouses. In this program, **five winners each receive a $10,000 grant** to boost their business. To be eligible, the company must be majority-owned by a veteran or spouse, have three to twenty employees, demonstrate financial need, and show a commitment to community impact. The application involves detailing your business plan and how you'd use the funds, and finalists may be asked to interview or provide additional documentation. This grant is competitive (hundreds apply), but it specifically honors businesses that exhibit the leadership and resilience qualities that veterans bring to entrepreneurship. Winners have

included childcare centers, fitness event companies, construction firms, and tech startups, reflecting the diversity of veteran-owned businesses.

- **Farmer Veteran Fellowship Fund** – For veterans going into agriculture or farming, the Farmer Veteran Coalition offers this fellowship grant. It provides small grants (typically $1,000 to $5,000) to help purchase equipment or supplies for farm businesses owned by veterans. To qualify, you must have an early-stage agriculture business and be a member of the **Farmer Veteran Coalition**. The application (which usually opens at the start of the year) requires an essay, business budget, and letters of recommendation. This grant is well-suited if you're transitioning from service to farming, helping cover startup costs like livestock, seeds, or minor infrastructure. It's not a huge sum of money, but for a small farm operation it can be a crucial boost to get started.
- **SBIR/STTR Research Grants** – If your business involves developing new technology or products, look into the **Small Business Innovation Research (SBIR)** and **Small Business Technology Transfer (STTR)** programs. These are federal grant programs (coordinated by the SBA) that fund R&D for small businesses in partnership with agencies like Defense, Energy, or Health. Many veteran-owned firms have successfully won SBIR/STTR grants to develop cutting-edge solutions (for example, in cybersecurity, biotech, or engineering). To be eligible, you must be a for-profit small business in the U.S. with under 500 employees, and proposing an innovative project that meets an agency's solicitation topic. The application process is intensive, you'll need to write a detailed proposal and typically have some technical expertise on your team. However, the payoff is significant: Phase I grants often range around $50,000–$250,000, and Phase II can exceed $1 million if your project shows promise. These grants are not limited to veterans, but as a veteran entrepreneur you may have an edge in defense-related

industries or by leveraging your military experience in the proposed research.

Finding and Applying: Beyond these specific programs, remember that databases like **Grants.gov** list thousands of grants from various government agencies. You can filter searches for veteran opportunities or see if agencies like the Department of Veterans Affairs or Department of Labor are offering small business grants in a given year. Additionally, platforms such as **GrantWatch** can help identify private grants for veterans (though they may require a subscription to get full details). Grant applications often require a solid business plan, evidence of your military service, and a clear explanation of how the funds will impact your venture. Start early and seek feedback on your grant proposals; resources like your local **Small Business Development Center (SBDC)** or a mentor can help you polish your submissions. While winning a grant is never guaranteed, the effort can be worthwhile for the chance at non-repayable capital to accelerate your business.

MENTORSHIP AND TRAINING PROGRAMS

One of the biggest advantages veteran entrepreneurs have available to them is access to a robust support ecosystem of mentorship, training, and networking programs. These resources can connect you with experienced entrepreneurs, help you refine your business skills, and even plug you into funding and customer networks. Leveraging such programs can greatly increase your odds of success. Here are some top mentorship and training avenues for veterans:

- **Bunker Labs** – Bunker Labs is a national network of veteran and military spouse entrepreneurs dedicated to helping the military community start and grow businesses. This 501(c)(3) nonprofit provides community, tools, and resources so that every veteran entrepreneur "has the network, tools, and resources they need" to thrive. Bunker Labs runs local chapters across the country, offering networking events (like "Bunker Brews"), online courses, and cohort-based programs. One flagship program is **Veterans in Residence**, a partnership with **WeWork/WeCompany** that provides co-working space and a six-month incubator for vet entrepreneurs. They also host pitch competitions and an annual showcase to connect vets with investors and business leaders. By joining Bunker Labs, you gain access to a peer community of veterans in business and mentors who understand the transition from the military. Many participants credit Bunker Labs with opening doors to partnerships and investors that they wouldn't have found otherwise.

- **Institute for Veterans and Military Families (IVMF)** – Housed at Syracuse University, IVMF is a leading academic institute offering entrepreneurship training for veterans and their families. Over the past decade, IVMF's programs have served over 200,000 veterans on their journey to business ownership. Notable programs include the **Entrepreneurship Bootcamp for Veterans (EBV),** an intensive multi-week training for post-9/11 veterans which combines online coursework with a residency at a partner university, and **V-WISE (Veteran Women Igniting the Spirit of Entrepreneurship)** for female veterans and military spouses. IVMF also offers **Boots to Business (B2B)** and **Boots to Business Reboot** in collaboration with the SBA, which are introductory two-day courses (part of the military Transition Assistance Program) to teach business fundamentals to those leaving service.

Recently, IVMF even acquired Bunker Labs to expand its offerings, meaning participants can tap into an even larger pool of programs and alumni networks. If you're looking for structured training (often at no cost to the veteran) and world-class entrepreneurship education,

IVMF programs are a goldmine. They often include long-term mentorship and access to resources like legal advice, small grants, or research libraries for veterans in business.

- **Veterans Business Outreach Centers (VBOCs)** – The SBA's Veterans Business Outreach Centers are a nationwide network of centers specifically set up to mentor and counsel veteran-owned small businesses. There are twenty-eight VBOCs across the country, and they offer free or low-cost workshops, one-on-one business counseling, and assistance with things like writing business plans or navigating SBA resources. For example, a VBOC might host a **Boots to Business** workshop on base, or help a veteran prepare a loan application package. If you're just starting out, your regional VBOC is an excellent first stop; they can assess your business idea, help you hone your strategy, and refer you to relevant programs (SBDCs, SCORE mentors, etc.) Many VBOC advisors are veterans or intimately familiar with veteran-specific programs, so they can tailor their advice to challenges like translating your military skills into business operations. You can locate your nearest center through the SBA website.
- **SCORE Mentors and SBDCs** – In addition to veteran-exclusive networks, don't overlook general small business resources that can be incredibly valuable. **SCORE** is a free mentorship program supported by SBA that connects entrepreneurs with experienced business mentors (many of whom are retired executives and a number are veterans themselves). They have a **Veteran Fast Launch Initiative** in some areas, and you can request a veteran mentor if that's important to you. **Small Business Development Centers (SBDC)** are another resource; these are local offices (often connected to universities or economic development agencies) providing free consulting on starting and growing a business. As a veteran, you can certainly use any SBDC, and often the SBDC will partner with the VBOC or veteran

organizations for events. For instance, a veteran in tech might get a SCORE mentor to help refine their business model and an SBDC advisor to assist with financial projections, a powerful combination of support. These mentorship resources provide ongoing guidance, accountability, and often help open doors to local opportunities or industry connections.

- **Veteran Business Networking Groups** – Beyond formal programs, there are numerous networking groups and incubators geared toward veteran entrepreneurs. For example, **Patriot Boot Camp** (originally backed by Techstars) is a startup accelerator for veterans and spouses that provides intensive training and an investor demo day. **Veterans Business Action Committee (VBAC)** in some regions (like Southern California) connects veteran business owners to mentor each other and influence local policy.

Industry-specific groups exist too, such as **VetFran** for those interested in franchising (providing discounts and mentorship to veteran franchisees), or **VetsinTech** for veterans in the technology startup scene. Engaging with these networks can provide camaraderie and valuable advice: fellow veterans can share how they raised capital, which banks or investors were "military friendly," and how to balance business with the residual challenges of transitioning to civilian life. Remember, as a veteran you're not alone in entrepreneurship; there's a whole community eager to help you succeed.

LESSONS FROM MY OWN BUSINESSES

As a veteran entrepreneur myself, I've learned firsthand how important these resources can be and I've also realized in hindsight where I could have leveraged them more. Let me share how some of the above programs and tools could have benefitted my own ventures, including **The Winfield Group Real Estate Team**, **Military Operated Real Estate (MORE)**, the **Enlisted Leadership Foundation**, and what I would do differently for **Inland Wharf Brewing Company** if I had the chance.

- **The Winfield Group Real Estate Team**– When I transitioned from the Navy and started The Winfield Group, a real estate team, I essentially bootstrapped the business while learning the ropes. In retrospect, an SBA Express loan or microloan could have accelerated our growth. For example, I could have used an **SBA Veterans Advantage loan** to invest in marketing and hire additional veteran agents early on, allowing us to scale faster. At the time, I wasn't aware that as an honorably discharged veteran I qualified for **fee-waived SBA loans**, had I applied, I might have secured affordable capital instead of relying solely on personal savings.

Additionally, tapping into mentorship networks like **SCORE** or **Bunker Labs** might have helped me develop more efficient systems from the get-go. Real estate is a relationship business, and organizations like Bunker Labs could have connected me with fellow veteran Realtors nationwide, potentially creating referral partnerships sooner. The lesson learned is not to try to "go it alone." Even though I eventually found success, I realize now that using the available veteran-focused resources from day one could have made the journey smoother and the growth trajectory steeper.

- **Enlisted Leadership Foundation (ELF)** – This is a nonprofit I've been heavily involved with, focused on providing leadership training to active-duty enlisted personnel. Running a nonprofit comes with its own set of challenges, distinct from for-profit ventures. We were fortunate to have a strong mission and community support, but I realize now that even nonprofits can benefit from the veteran business ecosystem. For instance, there are grants for veteran-driven community projects (sometimes via corporate foundations or state veteran affairs departments) that we could have pursued to fund our programs. Also, **mentorship programs** aren't just for businesses; I could have sought out a mentor who had grown a successful nonprofit to advise ELF on fundraising and scaling our courses. Organizations like the **Veterans Business Action Committee**, on which I serve, bring together seasoned veteran entrepreneurs who likely would have had valuable input on running ELF more like a "social enterprise."

Moreover, attending trainings like **Boots to Business Reboot** or the **Veteran Nonprofit Leadership** courses some universities offer could have provided insights into balancing our budget, marketing our events, and measuring impact. The lesson from ELF is that *leadership* in business also means continually learning; had we leveraged more veteran-focused networks, we might have discovered new partnerships or funding sources for our nonprofit much earlier. Any veteran starting a nonprofit should remember that many of the same business support tools (SBDCs, mentors, even SBA microloans in some cases) are available to you as well.

- **Inland Wharf Brewing Company** – My experience with Inland Wharf Brewing Co. is perhaps where hindsight is 20/20. This was a craft brewery I purchased, and while it was an exciting venture, we faced significant hurdles common in the food and beverage industry: high upfront capital needs for equipment, tight margins, and the challenge of building a brand in a crowded market. Looking back, I see a number of resources we could have leveraged differently. First and foremost, financing: we largely financed the brewery through personal funds and expensive credit, but we likely qualified for an **SBA 7(a)** or **504 loan** (since a brewery involves a lot of equipment and even real estate). An SBA 504 loan, for example, could have financed our brewing system and tasting room with a long-term, low-interest loan, preserving our cash flow. We also could have explored veteran-focused investor networks; there are angel investor groups that prefer veteran-led startups, and a brewery with a patriotic brand might have attracted interest if we had pitched at events like a **Veteran Shark Tank**.

Secondly, **mentorship and industry expertise**: neither my partner nor I had run a brewery before, and it showed in some of the trial-and-error we went through. I now know I could have reached out to SCORE to find a mentor from the food and beverage sector or even a fellow veteran who started a brewery. A candid mentor might have warned us about certain costly mistakes (like overproducing a style of beer that wasn't selling or signing a lease that was too expensive). Even joining a cohort of entrepreneurs through Bunker Labs or a local accelerator might have connected us to peers who could share advice. What would I have done differently? I would have written a detailed business plan and taken it to the VBOC/SBDC for feedback before launch, essentially, get a second set of eyes from experts. Then, I would have used that plan to pursue an SBA loan or attract investors, rather than under-capitalizing the business. I would have also attended more industry events (there are veteran business owner groups in craft brewing) to learn best practices. The hard lesson from Inland Wharf is that passion and hard work aren't always enough; you need adequate funding and a solid advisory network. If you're a veteran starting a brewery (or any business), take advantage of the loans, mentors, and training at your disposal; it could mean the difference between closing doors and lasting success.

- **Military Operated Real Estate (MORE)** – This venture is an extension of my real estate endeavors, aimed at building a network of military and veteran real estate professionals. The concept is to have an exclusive military affiliated team of highly trained Real Estate Agents, leveraging our military values and understanding of VA benefits to serve clients. I have taken all of the lessons learned and we are currently building this company with a MUCH stronger foundation than my previous ventures. **MORE,** is more than just a business; it's a mission-driven movement born out of my experience in both military service and real estate. This venture is a natural extension of my journey, combining the discipline, integrity, and commitment I developed in uniform with the entrepreneurial drive I've built in the civilian world. The core concept behind MORE is to create an elite, nationwide network of military-affiliated real estate professionals, veterans, active-duty service members, spouses, and dependents, who are uniquely positioned to understand and serve the housing needs of the military community. What sets MORE apart is not just our shared background, but our commitment to excellence through training, mentorship, and mission focus. Every agent in our network is required to undergo robust, standardized training that emphasizes the use of VA benefits, PCS planning, financial literacy, and real estate strategies tailored for military families. Our values aren't just slogans; they're lived experiences that shape how we lead, serve, and represent our clients.

I've taken every hard-earned lesson from my earlier ventures, the successes, failures, and everything in between, and used them to build this company on a far stronger foundation. This time, we're not just building a team; we're constructing an infrastructure designed for impact, sustainability, and scale. From legal compliance and referral systems to branding and strategic partnerships, MORE is being crafted with precision and purpose.

Our ultimate goal is to make MORE a trusted, household name for military homebuyers and sellers—much like USAA is for insurance or Navy Federal Credit Union is for banking. We believe our shared experiences give us the edge in empathy, expertise, and execution, and we're turning that into a real competitive advantage for the people we serve.

In summary, across all these ventures, I found that whenever I leveraged veteran resources, it paid off. And when I didn't, I often encountered avoidable hurdles. My advice to fellow veterans is to be *proactive* in seeking help. Our military culture sometimes teaches us to be self-reliant to a fault, but in entrepreneurship, asking for guidance or capital is a strength, not a weakness. Had I more fully utilized the arsenal of veteran entrepreneurship programs, I might have scaled bigger, faster, and with fewer bumps along the way.

SUCCESS STORIES AND CASE STUDIES

Nothing drives the point home better than real examples. Many veterans have built thriving businesses by tapping into the very loans, grants, and mentorship programs we've discussed. Here are a few success stories to illustrate how leveraging these resources can lead to business success:

Running Soles (Will Rivera) – Will Rivera, an Army veteran, turned his passion for running into a successful retail business with help from SBA programs. While still on active duty at Ft. Knox, Will took the **Boots to Business** entrepreneurship course and worked with an SBDC counselor to develop a business plan. Through that guidance, he secured an SBA-guaranteed loan in 2013 to open *Running Soles*, a specialty running shoe store. The store became a family-run business and a pillar of the community.

When the COVID-19 pandemic hit, Will once again leveraged SBA support by obtaining an Economic Injury Disaster Loan and a Paycheck Protection Program loan, which helped Running Soles cover expenses and keep employees on payroll during the downturn. By 2019, Will's venture was recognized as the Kentucky Veteran-Owned Small Business of the Year. His story shows how starting with the right training and financing (Boots to Business + SBA loan) set a strong foundation, and continuing to use available resources helped his business survive tough times. Veterans like Will prove that SBA programs can empower you to launch a brick-and-mortar business aligned with your passions.

Goodwin Facilities Solutions (Mitch Goodwin) – Mitch Goodwin is a service-disabled Army veteran who founded a construction and facilities management company. His journey highlights the power of combining training, counseling, and capital programs. Mitch attended an SBA-supported **Boots to Business** seminar through a Veterans Business Outreach Center, which he says was the push he needed to seriously pursue entrepreneurship. There he learned about registering as a **Service-Disabled Veteran-Owned Small Business (SDVOSB)** and the opportunities it opened in federal contracting. He then sought help from multiple SBA resource partners, the local SBDC and a Procurement Technical Assistance Center, to navigate government contracting and refine his business plan. With their assistance, Mitch also utilized SBA's loan guaranty programs to obtain financing for his company's growth.

Fast forward five years, **Goodwin Facilities Solutions** went from an idea to a thriving enterprise with roughly $12 million in government contract work on the books. Mitch's advice to other vets: "contact your local SBA office and go to one of these seminars…they gave me so many resources." His success demonstrates that veteran entrepreneurs who actively engage with SBA networks (training plus counseling plus loans) can break into lucrative markets, like federal contracting, and scale rapidly.

MyHome (Gabe and Lindsay Chrismon) – This husband-and-wife veteran duo had an innovative idea in the property management space and leveraged a veteran grant competition to jump-start their business. Gabe and Lindsay, both veterans, pitched their startup *MyHome* at **Warrior Rising's** annual veterans' business shower event in Salt Lake City. Thanks to a compelling business model and presentation, they won the first-place grant of $150,000, the largest ever awarded by Warrior Rising. This substantial infusion of capital is now propelling MyHome's growth. Beyond the money, by participating in Warrior Rising's program they also gained months of training and mentorship, helping them sharpen their business strategy.

Their story is a testament to the value of veteran-specific pitch competitions: not only can you secure funding without taking on debt or equity, but you also build confidence and networks. The Chrismons' success illustrates how preparing for and entering grant contests can validate your idea and provide critical resources. It's also inspiring to see veterans supporting veterans; the judges, mentors, and audience at Warrior Rising were all part of the community that wanted to see them win. If you have a strong business idea, following MyHome's example by engaging in a veteran entrepreneurship incubator or contest could be your springboard to success.

These case studies underscore a common theme: veterans who *actively seek out and use* the programs designed for us tend to thrive. Whether it's training plus an SBA loan to open a local business, comprehensive counseling plus financing to build a contracting company, or competition training plus grants to launch a startup, the resources are out there and proven to work.

As a veteran entrepreneur, you have an entire ecosystem ready to invest in your success, from government agencies to nonprofit foundations and fellow veterans who have walked the path before. The most important step is to reach out and take advantage of these opportunities. Use the lessons from those who succeeded: plan diligently, as Marine vet, Fred Smith of FedEx, emphasized, "great planning is absolutely essential for an aspiring entrepreneur," leverage your military-honed grit and leadership; and don't hesitate to utilize every veteran program available. By doing so, you put yourself in the best position to build a thriving business in civilian life.

In conclusion, starting a veteran-owned business is challenging, but you have a wealth of support that civilians often lack. Take the initiative to research loans and grants you qualify for, get involved in the veteran entrepreneur community, and learn from both your peers and mentors. Combine your military discipline with these resources to maximize your chances of success. The goal is to work *smarter,* not just harder, by using the tools at your disposal. With smart planning, adequate funding, continuous learning, and a supportive network, you can navigate the entrepreneurial battlefield and emerge victorious, just as many fellow veterans have. Good luck on your mission of entrepreneurship, and remember, you're fighting for your own success now, but you're never fighting alone.

BUILDING PASSIVE INCOME BEFORE YOU SEPARATE

One of the smartest financial moves you can make before leaving the military is to start building **passive income streams,** so that when you transition, you're not relying 100% on a paycheck from your next job. Too many service members wait until their final year of service to start thinking about income outside of their military salary. The result? A stressful scramble for employment post-separation.

Instead, your goal should be to set up income-generating assets while you're still in uniform, allowing you to leave the military with multiple streams of revenue already working for you. The key to passive income is making your money, time, or knowledge work for you, so you're not trading hours for dollars.

Here are some of the best ways to build passive income while still in the military:

1. Real Estate Investments: Using VA Home Loans to Build a Rental Portfolio

You already know my thoughts on real estate: it's one of the fastest and most effective ways to build long-term wealth. If you start buying properties at each duty station and renting them out when you move, you could retire from the military with multiple cash-flowing properties that provide income for life.

Use Your VA Home Loan Smartly – Buy a duplex, triplex, or quadplex and live in one unit while renting out the others. Refer back to the section on house hacking for more details.

PCS-Proof Your Properties – Instead of selling when you move, rent it out. Military bases always have built-in demand for rentals, as incoming service members need housing fast.

Take Advantage of the SCRA – As mentioned previously, if you rent your property for up to thirteen years after moving due to PCS orders, you still qualify for the capital gains tax exemption when you sell. That means up to $500,000 in profit (if married) is tax-free.

Leverage Property Management – If you don't want to manage tenants, hire a property manager. They'll handle the day-to-day tasks while you collect passive rental income.

By the time you leave the military, even if you only purchase one property every few years, you could have a portfolio of three to five properties generating thousands of dollars in passive income every month.

2. Dividend Stocks & Passive Investment Accounts

Stock market investing is another excellent hands-off way to build passive income over time. By consistently investing a portion of every paycheck into dividend-paying stocks or index funds, you create an income stream that grows even after you leave the military.

Dividend Stocks – These stocks pay you a percentage of their profits every quarter (or sometimes monthly). Over time, those dividend payments can become a reliable income source.

Automatic Investments – Set up automatic contributions to a brokerage account, Roth IRA, or TSP while you're still in uniform. The earlier you start, the more you benefit from compound interest.

Real Estate Investment Trusts (REITs) – If you don't want to manage rental properties, REITs allow you to invest in real estate without actually owning property. These funds pay high dividends, making them a great passive income tool.

If you start investing even just $200 per month in dividend-paying stocks while in the military, by the time you transition, you could be earning hundreds (or thousands) of dollars per month in dividends.

3. Online Businesses & Digital Products

More and more veterans are building online businesses that generate passive income, even while they're still serving. The great thing about digital businesses is that they can be run from anywhere and often require little overhead.

Affiliate Marketing – Promote products and services online and earn commission-based passive income whenever someone makes a purchase.

E-commerce & Drop shipping – Sell products online without handling inventory. Platforms like Shopify, Amazon FBA, and Etsy allow you to start an online store with little upfront cost.

Create Digital Products – Sell eBooks, courses, templates, or training programs online. Once created, these products generate income on autopilot.

YouTube & Podcasting – Some veterans turn their military experience, financial knowledge, or fitness expertise into video or audio content that earns passive income through ads, sponsorships, and memberships.

The beauty of online businesses is that once you build them, they continue to make money even when you're not actively working.

Start small while in uniform, and by the time you separate, you could have a self-sustaining income stream.

4. VA Disability Compensation & Pensions – A Built-In Passive Income Stream

If you leave the military with a service-connected disability, VA disability compensation can become a major source of passive income. Below is the compensation as of 2025.

2025 VA Disability Compensation Rates (Veteran Alone)

DISABILITY RATING

Disability Rating	Monthly Payment
10%	$175.51
20%	$346.95
30%	$537.42
40%	$774.16
50%	$1,102.04
60%	$1,395.93
70%	$1,759.19
80%	$2,044.89
90%	$2,297.96
100%	$3,831.30

Note: Veterans with a 10% or 20% disability rating do not receive additional compensation for dependents.

Additional Compensation for Dependents (30%–100% Ratings)

If your disability rating is 30% or higher, you may be eligible for additional monthly compensation based on your number of dependents

- **Spouse**: Additional amount varies by rating
- **Children under Eighteen**: Additional amount per child
- **Children over Eighteen in school**: Additional amount per child
- **Dependent parents**: Additional amount per parent
- **Spouse receiving Aid and Attendance**: Additional amount varies by rating

For exact amounts, refer to the VA's official compensation tables or consult with a VA representative.

Many veterans don't realize they're eligible for disability benefits and fail to file their claims before separation. If you wait too long, you risk losing out on years of potential income.

Start your VA claims process at least twelve months before you leave the military. Get a VSO (Veteran Service Officer) to help you submit your claim properly so you maximize your benefits.

While real estate, investing, and online businesses may take time to build, VA benefits provide an immediate passive income cushion while you grow your other revenue streams.

Passive Income = Financial Freedom in Civilian Life

By building multiple streams of income while you're still serving, you set yourself up for financial freedom and security when you transition.

Real Estate – Own properties that generate rental income

Dividend Stocks – Invest in assets that pay you quarterly

Online Business – Create digital income streams that run themselves

VA Benefits – Lock in compensation that provides financial stability

The best time to start building passive income is NOW, while you still have a steady paycheck, housing benefits, and low financial risk. By the time you separate, you could be in a position where you never have to stress about money again, because your passive income covers your bills before you even start your civilian career. And that's the goal: to transition with confidence, not fear.

FINAL THOUGHTS: SET YOURSELF UP FOR FINANCIAL SUCCESS

The transition from military to civilian life doesn't have to be stressful. If you plan ahead and take advantage of the benefits and resources available, you can step into financial security, independence, and even wealth.

Start building passive income streams now—before you separate. Use SkillBridge or an apprenticeship program to gain real-world experience while still in uniform. If entrepreneurship is your path, take advantage of veteran-focused business resources and mentorship programs.

But mindset isn't enough—you need a tactical plan. Here's your Transition Toolkit to help you prepare:

- Submit your VA disability claim as early as possible.
- Set up your LinkedIn profile and start networking in your target industry.
- Enroll in TAP (Transition Assistance Program) early and attend every session.
- Meet with a financial planner to evaluate your post-military income and expenses.
- Explore SkillBridge, VA-backed education, and career certifications.
- Rebuild your budget for civilian life—based on your new income, not your LES.

The military trained you to plan for the mission—this next chapter is no different. With the right preparation, your transition can be the launchpad to a stronger financial future.

I hear and forget. What I write I understand.

TWELVE
LIFE INSURANCE & PROTECTING YOUR LEGACY

THE ONE THING WE ALL AVOID TALKING ABOUT

I KNOW we touched on this in previous chapters but let's dive a little deeper so let's be real: no one likes to talk about life insurance. It's not exactly the most thrilling topic, and most of us don't wake up in the morning thinking, *"Wow, today is a great day to discuss what happens when I die!"* But here's the deal: if you don't plan for it, your family is the one that pays the price.

As military families, we plan for deployments, PCS moves, retirement, and even where to stash our emergency stash of MREs, but too many of us don't plan for the inevitable. And that's a problem. I'll be honest; I didn't think much about life insurance early in my career. I had SGLI, and I figured, *Hey, I'm covered!* But as I started to learn more about financial security, I realized that SGLI is just the bare minimum.

The hard truth? If something happened to me, I didn't just want my family to be "fine," I wanted them to be financially secure for life. That's when I started looking into how to use life insurance as a financial tool, not just a safety net. And let me tell you, it's a game-changer.

WHY MILITARY FAMILIES NEED TO RETHINK LIFE INSURANCE

Most service members assume that SGLI is enough. And while $500,000 sounds like a lot, here's what happens when you break it down:

Taxes & Expenses – While SGLI is tax-free, funeral expenses, debts, and immediate costs can eat into that payout.

Lost Income – If you're the primary breadwinner, your family will need a long-term income replacement, not just a one-time check.

Kids' Education & Future Needs – $500K may seem like plenty, but college tuition, mortgage payments, and daily living expenses add up fast.

That's when I realized that having additional life insurance is not about fear; it's about responsibility. It's about making sure my family never has to struggle.

TURNING LIFE INSURANCE INTO A FINANCIAL TOOL

Most people see life insurance as just a policy that pays out when you die, but wealthy people use it as a financial tool while they're still alive.

Whole **Life & Indexed Universal Life Insurance (IULs)** – These policies build cash value, which means you can borrow against them like a personal bank.

Tax-**Free Wealth Transfer** – Life insurance payouts are tax-free, making it one of the best ways to pass down wealth.

Retirement **Planning** – Some life insurance policies allow you to withdraw from the cash value as an extra retirement fund.

I realized that the right life insurance policy could actually help me build wealth, not just protect my family. So, here's the bottom line: life insurance isn't just about preparing for the worst; it's about securing the best future for your loved ones. If you haven't taken the time to understand your options, now is the time. Because the worst thing you can do is wait until it's too late.

WHY LIFE INSURANCE MATTERS FOR MILITARY FAMILIES

Military families face unique financial risks. We move frequently, our spouses often sacrifice careers to follow us, and we're constantly juggling uncertainty. Life insurance is the ultimate backup plan to make sure your loved ones are financially stable, no matter what.

Here's why it's critical:

Income Replacement – If something happens to you, your family still has a source of income

Covers Mortgage & Debts – Keeps your family in their home and out of financial hardship

Pays for Kids' Education – Ensures your kids don't have to struggle to afford school.

Legacy Building – Provides generational wealth instead of just covering funeral cost

Let's be real: if you've spent twenty plus years in uniform, you probably want to leave your family with more than just a DD-214 and some old war stories.

UNDERSTANDING TERM VS. WHOLE LIFE INSURANCE

There are two main types of life insurance: **Term** and **Whole Life**. Each serves a purpose, but one has a secret wealth-building component that most people don't understand.

1. Term Life Insurance – The Budget Option

Term life insurance is straightforward and affordable: you pay a premium, and if you die within the term (typically ten to thirty years), your family gets a payout. But if you outlive the term, the policy disappears like that E-3 who suddenly "had duty" when it was time to clean the barracks.

Affordable – monthly payments are cheap, making it ideal for young service members

High Coverage for Low Cost – you can get a large death benefit for a low premium

No Cash Value – if you outlive the policy, you get nothing (which means the insurance company wins)

Temporary – once the term expires, you either lose coverage or pay a much higher premium to renew

Who Should Get Term Life?

If you're looking for basic, affordable protection to cover your family's financial needs (like replacing your income or covering a mortgage), term life is the way to go. But if you want something more than just a death benefit, keep reading.

2. Whole Life Insurance – The Wealth-Building Tool

Whole life insurance is more than just a payout when you die, it's a financial asset. Unlike term life, it builds cash value over time that you can borrow against, invest, or even use for retirement.

When I first heard about this, I thought it was a financial scam. I mean, life insurance as a wealth-building tool? But when I started digging deeper, I realized that the rich have been using this strategy forever.

HOW I USED MY LIFE INSURANCE TO BE MY OWN BANK

One of the most powerful aspects of whole life insurance is that you can borrow against your own policy's cash value, instead of taking out high-interest loans from banks. This clicked for me when I needed to invest in my businesses. Instead of going through banks, credit checks, and high-interest rates, I borrowed against my own policy.

Here's why this strategy is genius:

You Pay Yourself Back with Interest – Instead of making the banks richer, you grow your own wealth by repaying yourself.

No Credit Check or Approval Process – Need cash? Borrow from your policy: no bank, no waiting, no questions asked.

Tax-Free Growth – The cash value grows tax-free, and you can withdraw strategically without penalties.

Guaranteed Growth – Unlike risky investments, whole life insurance cash value grows at a stable rate.

I personally used this strategy to help fund The Winfield Group and Military Operated Real Estate (MORE). Instead of taking out a high-interest loan, I borrowed from my policy, invested the money, paid myself back, and built wealth, all at the same time. And here's the kicker: you can use this strategy to buy real estate, start a business, or even fund your retirement.

Pro Tip: Start Early & Build Your Financial Fortress

If you start a whole life policy in your twenties or thirties, the cash value can become a financial powerhouse by the time you retire. Many people don't realize this, but some of the wealthiest families in America have been using life insurance as a tax-free generational wealth strategy for decades. So, if you're thinking long-term and want both financial security AND an investment tool, whole life insurance is worth considering.

USING TRUSTS TO PROTECT YOUR WEALTH

Having life insurance is a great first step, but if you really want to protect your wealth and legacy, you need to take it a step further and set up a trust. A trust isn't just for the ultra-rich, it's for anyone who wants to ensure their hard-earned assets are protected from legal battles, unnecessary taxes, and financial mismanagement.

Why You Need a Trust

Think of a trust as a financial safety vault: a legal entity that holds your assets and distributes them exactly how you want when you're gone.

Your Life Insurance Payout is Protected – If you don't have a trust, your life insurance money could get stuck in probate, delaying payments to your family. A trust ensures the money is quickly and smoothly distributed.

Your Assets Go to the Right People – Without a trust, family disputes and court battles can arise over who gets what. A trust removes any confusion and guarantees your assets are distributed according to your wishes.

Your Children or Dependents Are Secure – If something happens to you, a trust controls how and when your children receive money, ensuring they don't blow through an inheritance or get taken advantage of. You can set rules, like distributing funds only for college, housing, or after they reach a certain age.

You Avoid Unnecessary Taxes – The right type of trust can reduce estate taxes, preventing Uncle Sam from taking a huge chunk of your hard-earned wealth.

TYPES OF TRUSTS FOR LIFE INSURANCE & WEALTH PROTECTION

Each type of trust serves a different purpose, and the right one depends on your goals.

1. Revocable Living Trust – Maximum Flexibility

A Revocable Living Trust allows you to retain control over your assets while you're alive. You can change beneficiaries, update instructions, or move assets in and out of the trust.

Best for: people who want **flexibility** and **full control** of their assets until they pass away

Downside: assets in a **revocable trust are still subject to estate taxes** after death

2. Irrevocable Life Insurance Trust (ILIT) – Tax Protection

An ILIT is a powerful tool for anyone using life insurance as part of their wealth strategy. It takes ownership of your life insurance policy, meaning the payout is NOT counted as part of your taxable estate.

Removes life insurance from your taxable estate

Ensures responsible distribution of funds

Provides long-term wealth protection for your heirs

Best for: people with large life insurance policies who want to avoid estate taxes and ensure payouts are used responsibly. Large life insurance policies who want to avoid estate taxes

Downside: once you set up an ILIT, you can't change it; it's locked in

3. Testamentary Trust – Included in Your Will

A **Testamentary Trust** is created as part of your will and only takes effect after you pass away. This allows you to specify exactly how and when your assets should be distributed.

Best for: People who want to ensure their kids or dependents receive money responsibly over time

Downside: Because it only activates after death, it still has to go through probate, which can cause delays and legal costs

REAL-WORLD EXAMPLE: PROTECTING YOUR FAMILY'S FUTURE

Let's say you have a $1 million life insurance policy and two young kids. Without a trust:

The payout goes directly to your estate, potentially getting tied up in probate and subject to taxes.

If your kids are under eighteen, the court decides how the money is handled until they turn eighteen, at which point they get a lump sum (which isn't always a good thing).

With a trust:

- The payout avoids probate, so your family gets the money immediately
- You set rules for distribution; for example, your kids get 25% at twenty-one, 25% at twenty-five, and the rest at thirty (instead of blowing it all at eighteen)
- You ensure the money is used for education, housing, or other financial needs, rather than being wasted

Pro Tip: Meet with an Estate Planner

A trust isn't one-size-fits-all, so it's important to work with an estate planner or attorney to set up the right trust for your situation. They can help you:

Decide which trust structure fits your goals

Ensure your real estate, life insurance, and investments are properly protected

Minimize taxes and legal headaches for your beneficiaries

Bottom Line: If you want to ensure your wealth is protected and passed down properly, setting up a trust is one of the smartest moves you can make. Don't wait until it's too late: plan now and give your family the security they deserve.

FINAL THOUGHTS: PROTECT YOUR FAMILY AND BUILD WEALTH

If you have dependents, you NEED life insurance, no excuses

Term life is great for protection, whole life is great for wealth-building

If you start early, you can use life insurance as your own bank

A trust ensures your assets go to the right people, tax-efficiently

Your military benefits (SGLI) won't last forever, plan ahead

Life insurance isn't just about what happens when you die; it's about protecting your family and building financial freedom while you're alive.

I hear and forget. What I write I understand.

THIRTEEN
FINANCIAL INDEPENDENCE & RETIREMENT PLANNING FOR VETERANS

THE RETIREMENT WAKE-UP CALL

YOU HAVE HEARD me say it before, one of the biggest misconceptions among service members is assuming military retirement pay is enough to live comfortably. Spoiler alert: It's not.

I remember talking to a retired senior chief who told me, *"I thought my pension would be plenty, until I actually retired."* Turns out, after taxes, health care costs, inflation, and everyday expenses, that pension didn't stretch nearly as far as he expected. Instead of kicking back and enjoying retirement, he found himself scrambling to find another job just to maintain the same quality of life he had while on active duty.

WHY MILITARY RETIREMENT PAY ALONE ISN'T ENOUGH

Here's the reality:

Military retirement pay is based on your base pay, not your full paycheck. That means no more BAH or BAS once you retire.

Taxes take a bigger bite. Depending on where you live, your pension is taxed at the state and federal level, reducing your take-home amount.

Health care costs increase significantly. While **TRICARE for Life** and VA benefits help, out-of-pocket medical expenses (especially for families) can add up fast.

Inflation eats away at your purchasing power. The cost of living increases every year, and your pension won't always keep up.

For example, let's say you retire as an E-7 with twenty years of service.

Your estimated monthly retirement pay: **around $2,500–$3,000**

After taxes and deductions: **closer to $2,000–$2,500 take-home**

Cost of rent or mortgage? **Gone**

Health care premiums and co-pays? **New reality**

Inflation? **Killing your spending power year after year**

When you break it down, that pension isn't the financial security blanket many think it is.

THE GOOD NEWS: YOU CAN PREPARE NOW

The best way to avoid financial stress in retirement is to start planning long before you hang up your uniform.

Build Multiple Income Streams – Passive income through real estate, dividends, and side businesses can supplement your pension.

Maximize TSP and Investments – Contribute aggressively to your TSP and roll it into high-yield investments when you retire.

Own Instead of Rent – If you buy real estate at each duty station, you could have multiple rental properties generating income by retirement.

Understand VA Disability Benefits – Many veterans qualify for VA disability pay, which is tax-free and can significantly boost retirement income.

Have a Post-Military Plan – Whether it's starting a business, leveraging SkillBridge, or entering a high-paying civilian career, having a strategy before retirement ensures you're not caught off guard.

RETIRE FINANCIALLY STRONG, NOT JUST RETIRED

You don't want to spend twenty plus years serving your country only to struggle financially after leaving. The key to a stress-free military retirement is building financial independence while you're still in uniform.

The bottom line? Your pension alone won't cut it, but with the right financial moves, you'll never have to work another job unless you want to. Let's break down exactly how to retire from the military financially strong and ready for civilian life.

Step 1: Define Your Retirement Vision

Retirement isn't just about not working—it's about having the freedom to live life on your terms. Whether that means kicking back and relaxing or launching into your next big venture, your financial plan needs to support your vision.

Ask yourself:

Do you want to travel the world, exploring new places without financial worry?

Do you want to start a business and be your own boss?

Do you want to buy a home and settle down, living mortgage-free?

Do you want to work part-time, not because you have to, but because you enjoy staying busy?

Your answers will determine how much money you actually need to retire comfortably.

RETIREMENT REALITY CHECK

A veteran who wants to live in a paid-off house in a low-cost state will need a very different financial plan than someone who wants to live in downtown San Diego and take European vacations every year.

Lesson Learned: When I left active duty, I thought my military pension and VA disability pay would be enough, until I actually ran the numbers. That's when I realized I needed multiple income streams to retire stress-free and maintain the lifestyle I wanted.

Step 2: Maximize Your Military Benefits

The military provides some of the best retirement benefits available, but too many veterans fail to take full advantage of them. Leaving benefits on the table is like turning down free money, don't make that mistake.

Blended Retirement System (BRS) – If you're still serving, make sure you're contributing at **least 5% to your TSP** to get the full government match; that's free money!

VA Disability Compensation – If you haven't filed a VA claim yet, do it **NOW**. VA disability pay is tax-free, and even a 10-30% rating can significantly supplement your income.

Tricare for Life – If eligible, Tricare provides low-cost health care in retirement, saving you thousands compared to private insurance. Health care costs will be one of your biggest expenses; plan ahead.

Survivor Benefit Plan (SBP) – If you have dependents, consider whether SBP makes sense for your family's long-term security. It's a lifeline for many spouses who would otherwise lose pension benefits.

Lesson Learned: I saw too many veterans ignore their VA benefits until they desperately needed them. Filing for disability after you retire is much harder; get your claim done early so you're set up for success.

Step 3: Build Multiple Income Streams

Relying only on military retirement pay is risky, especially with inflation and rising costs. To truly achieve financial independence, you need multiple sources of income so you're not stressed about money after leaving the military.

Here's how you can start building wealth before and after retirement:

1. Invest in Real Estate

Use your VA Home Loan to buy investment properties while you're still in uniform.

House Hack – Buy a multi-unit property, live in one unit, rent out the others to cover your mortgage.

Keep properties when you PCS – If you buy a home at every duty station, you could retire with multiple cash-flowing rental properties.

Lesson Learned: I wish I had bought a home at every PCS move, I'd have an entire real estate portfolio by now.

2. Invest in Stocks & Retirement Accounts

Max out your TSP and Roth IRA while on active duty

Invest in dividend-paying stocks for passive income

Consider tax-advantaged accounts like Roth IRAs to grow tax-free wealth

Lesson Learned: If I had started investing just $100 a month into an S&P 500 index fund when I was an E-5, I'd have hundreds of thousands of dollars by now. Start early!

3. Start a Business or Side Hustle

Consider starting a veteran-owned business using SBA loans or grants

Monetize your skills, whether it's consulting, coaching, or digital products

Use SkillBridge or apprenticeship programs before you retire to test the waters in a new industry

Lesson Learned: My first business outside of real estate, Inland Wharf Brewing Company, failed, but it taught me invaluable lessons that helped me build The Winfield Group and MORE into successful ventures. Failure isn't the end; it's part of the process.

Step 4: Reduce Expenses & Plan for Taxes

Even if you have multiple income streams, poor financial management can ruin a great retirement plan. Here's how to keep more of your money:

Eliminate Debt Before Retirement – The less you owe, the more financial flexibility you'll have

Live Within Your Means – If your pension is $3,000 a month, don't take on a $4,000 mortgage

Understand Taxes on Military Retirement Pay – Some states tax military pensions, while others don't. Choosing a tax-friendly state can save you thousands

Lesson Learned: I used to think making more money was the answer, until I realized keeping more of what I make is just as important. Smart tax and debt planning will set you up for success.

Step 5: Set Up a Retirement Blueprint

A financial independence plan isn't just about hoping everything works out; it's about having a clear and actionable strategy before you retire.

One Year Before Retirement:

- **Lock in your VA Disability claim**
- **Decide where you want to live**
- **Start networking for post-military job or business opportunities**
- **Pay off as much debt as possible**

Six Months Before Retirement:

- **Apply for Tricare or other healthcare coverage**
- **Set up a plan for your TSP, IRA, and other investments**
- **Ensure you have multiple income streams lined up**

Final Ninety Days:

- **Get your estate planning done (trusts, wills, etc.)**
- **Review your budget for post-military life**
- **Execute your transition plan!**

Lesson Learned: Too many veterans wing it when they retire, but a solid plan makes all the difference. Having a retirement blueprint ensures you don't just survive after service: you thrive.

RETIRE ON YOUR TERMS

The military may have structured your career, but your retirement is up to you. With the right planning, you can leave service financially strong, debt-free, and fully in control of your future.

The key? Start NOW. The sooner you take action, the better your financial future will be.

FINAL THOUGHTS: RETIREMENT IS JUST THE BEGINNING

Retirement pay is NOT enough on its own. Plan ahead and treat retirement not as the finish line—but as your next starting point.

Invest in real estate, stocks, and businesses to build reliable passive income. Maximize your VA benefits and military retirement resources, but don't rely on them to carry you without a plan. Have a clear, step-by-step approach for your post-military financial life.

Here's a quick **Retirement Checklist** to help you assess your readiness:

- What will your total income be post-retirement (pension, VA, investments)?
- Have you accounted for taxes, inflation, and loss of housing allowances?
- Do you have a plan to supplement income—through a business, real estate, or part-time work?
- Will your home be paid off, or will you still owe rent or a mortgage?
- What's your strategy for healthcare, life insurance, and college savings?

The goal isn't just to retire from the military; it's to retire financially free—with options, flexibility, and long-term security.

In the next chapter, we'll bring it all together: The Final *Military, Money, and MORE* Blueprint.

I hear and forget. What I write I understand.

FOURTEEN
THE MILITARY, MONEY, AND MORE BLUEPRINT

FINANCIAL FREEDOM IS A MISSION – TREAT IT LIKE ONE

WHEN WE WERE in the military, every mission had a plan, an objective, and a set of orders to follow. Whether it was preparing for deployment, qualifying on a weapons range, or executing operations at sea, success depended on discipline, preparation, and execution.

Financial freedom is no different, it's a mission.

The problem? Most service members don't get a set of financial orders when they raise their right hand and take the oath. No one hands you a financial readiness manual during boot camp. Instead, we're left to figure it out on our own, often by trial and error. I had to learn the hard way.

I made plenty of financial mistakes: taking out the wrong kind of mortgage, racking up insane amount of debt, starting businesses without a plan, and thinking I could just work harder to make up for bad money decisions. But here's the thing: **you can't outwork bad financial habits.**

For years, I thought if I just hustled harder, if I picked up more clients, if I worked sixty-hour weeks, I'd be able to outrun my financial problems. But no matter how much money I made, I always seemed to be catching up, not getting ahead. Sound familiar? What I eventually realized is that financial security isn't about luck; it's about following a blueprint. The same way we train for missions, we need to train for financial independence. And just like in the military, you don't have to go at it alone.

That's why I built Military Operated Real Estate (MORE); not just as a real estate company, but as a financial education movement designed to give service members, veterans, and military families the tools, knowledge, and community support to build generational wealth. **It's not just about making money; it's about having a mission for your money.**

And just like any mission, success starts with a plan. So, here's your financial mission briefing: a step-by-step action plan to take control of your financial future and never have to stress about money again.

The objective? Financial freedom

The enemy? Debt, bad financial habits, and wasted opportunities

The strategy? Invest smart, leverage military benefits, and build long-term wealth

This is your financial mission: execute it with the same discipline, focus, and determination that made you successful in the military.

ACTION PLAN FOR VETERANS AND MILITARY FAMILIES

Here's your mission briefing for taking control of your money, eliminating debt, and building long-term wealth.

1. Budget and Track Spending

Let's start with the basics: if you don't know where your money is going, you're already losing the battle.

Track every dollar. Whether it's an app, a spreadsheet, or old-school pen and paper, know where your money is going.

Identify wasteful spending. If your morning Starbucks run is costing you $200 a month, it's time for a reality check.

Create a spending plan. Every mission has an operational plan, your money should too.

Lesson learned: Early in my career, I thought making more money was the answer. But every time I got a pay raise, I increased my spending, not my savings. Until I built a budget, I was just treading water financially.

2. Build an Emergency Fund

Most Americans, including service members, don't have $1,000 in savings for an emergency. That's a problem.

Aim for three to six months of living expenses saved. This is your financial body armor.

Keep it liquid. This isn't an investment, it's cash set aside for emergencies.

Start small if necessary. Even saving $50 a paycheck adds up over time.

Lesson learned: I used to think an "emergency fund" was for rich people. But after maxing out credit cards to cover unexpected expenses, I realized that having cash reserves is the difference between financial stability and financial chaos.

3. Eliminate High-Interest Debt

Debt is the financial equivalent of carrying a rucksack full of bricks; it weighs you down and slows your progress. The first step to financial freedom is lightening the load.

Prioritize paying off credit cards first. These have the highest interest rates and keep you trapped in the cycle.

Use the debt snowball or avalanche method. Pick a strategy and attack debt aggressively.

Stop borrowing money for things you don't need. If you can't afford it without a credit card, you can't afford it.

Lesson learned: I once thought balance transfers and minimum payments were "managing" my debt. Nope. Turns out, I was just kicking the can down the road. When I finally focused on paying debt off aggressively, my entire financial outlook changed.

4. Maximize Military Benefits

The military provides some of the best financial benefits available, but too many service members don't take full advantage of them.

Use your VA Home Loan to buy property. Don't waste money renting when you could be building equity.

Invest in your TSP or Roth IRA. Even if you start with just $100 a month, get that compound interest working for you.

Take advantage of SkillBridge or Apprenticeship programs. Get paid to learn a new career before you separate.

Lesson learned: I ignored my TSP for years—big mistake. If I had maxed it out early, I would've had a six-figure investment account before leaving the military.

5. Invest Early & Often

Investing is how wealth is built. Period.

Start NOW. The earlier you invest, the more time your money has to grow.

Automate investments. Set it and forget it. Every paycheck should include an investment contribution.

Diversify. Real estate, index funds, and whole life insurance all play a role in a solid investment strategy.

Lesson learned: I used to think investing was risky. But the real risk? Not investing at all.

6. Own Real Estate

We've covered this before, but it's worth repeating: **real estate is one of the best ways to build wealth.**

Buy a home instead of renting. Every PCS move is an opportunity to own an appreciating asset.

Use your VA Home Loan multiple times. Don't stop at one home: build a portfolio.

House hack. Rent out rooms or buy multi-unit properties to live for free.

Lesson learned: If I had started buying a home at every duty station, I'd have a real estate empire by now.

7. Leverage VA Resources for Financial Growth

The VA has more resources than most veterans realize.

VA Small Business Loans – If you want to start a business, the VA helps veterans secure funding.

VA Education Benefits – Don't just use your GI Bill for school, use it for certifications and job training.

VA Health Care & Disability Benefits – Take care of your health AND your wallet.

Lesson learned: VA resources helped me start businesses, invest in real estate, and build financial security. Use them!

A CALL TO ACTION – JOIN THE MORE COMMUNITY

You don't have to figure this out alone. The MORE community is here to help veterans and military families achieve financial freedom.

Learn from those who've been there.

Surround yourself with financially smart veterans.

Take action—don't just read about financial freedom, go get it!

The mission isn't over when you leave the military; it's just beginning. Financial freedom is possible, but you must make it your mission.

FINAL THOUGHTS: YOUR MISSION ISN'T OVER—IT'S JUST CHANGING

You've served your country with honor, discipline, and sacrifice. Now it's time to serve your future with the same level of commitment. Financial freedom isn't a dream—it's a mission. And like every mission, success requires preparation, strategy, and execution.

You don't need to know everything. You just need to start.

- Start tracking your money.
- Start investing in your future.
- Start using the benefits you've earned.
- Start leading your family toward financial security.

You are the commander now. This is your op order for life beyond the uniform.

So, here's your final directive: Stop waiting. Start now.

Let this book be the foundation—but let your action be the legacy.

Now go out and build your legacy!!!

I hear and forget. What I write I understand.

BONUS CHAPTER: REAL VETERAN STORIES OF WEALTH AND FINANCIAL STRUGGLES

FINANCIAL ADVICE IS POWERFUL—BUT it becomes transformational when paired with real stories. This bonus chapter compiles the financial journeys of U.S. service members and veterans who overcame debt, built wealth, and leveraged military benefits. Whether you're stationed at your first duty post or transitioning out, these stories reflect your reality—and your potential. *This chapter is based on publicly available stories from credible news outlets, government programs, and nonprofit organizations. These accounts are paraphrased and contextualized to educate and inspire service members and veterans. All stories are attributed to their original sources. See "Notes & References" at the end of this chapter.*

ERICKA SMITH (NAVY VETERAN) – FROM $25K IN CREDIT CARD DEBT TO FINANCIAL PEACE

Challenge: Ericka Smith, a Navy veteran based in Washington State, found herself drowning in over $25,000 of credit card debt after her marriage ended. The financial issues weren't sudden; they were years in the making. Ericka and her spouse had never discussed a budget or long-term financial goals. They lived in the moment, often spending money they didn't have, believing the next paycheck would cover their needs. The rising cost of living, including groceries, rent, and child care, only compounded their poor financial habits. By the time the divorce was finalized, Ericka was left with not only emotional wounds but also a financial hole that seemed impossible to escape.

Strategy: The divorce served as a wake-up call. Ericka realized she had to face the reality of her financial life. For the first time, she sat down and made a budget. She listed every single debt and created a strict repayment plan. She cut out nearly all non-essential expenses; no more dining out, shopping sprees, or premium streaming services. She cooked at home, cancelled subscriptions, and even sold a few items she no longer used. Every spare dollar went toward her debt. To stay motivated, she tracked her progress monthly and gave herself small wins, like celebrating each $1,000 paid off. Importantly, she also sought out community support by attending local budgeting workshops and engaging with online groups focused on financial recovery.

Outcome: Within a year, Ericka made major headway. Her credit card balances were slashed significantly, and the stress that once kept her up at night began to subside. She wasn't fully out of debt yet, but for the first time, she felt in control of her money. Today, she operates on a structured budget, lives within her means, and uses credit responsibly. She even set up a savings account—something she hadn't done in years. The transformation wasn't just financial; it was emotional and mental. Ericka now describes her lifestyle as peaceful, empowered, and sustainable.

Lesson: Financial healing starts with brutal honesty. Ericka's story teaches that no matter how deep your debt or how long you've ignored it, it's never too late to take back control. Her transformation also underscores the importance of communication, whether with a partner or with oneself. Budgeting, intentional living, and accountability can radically shift your financial trajectory—even after a crisis.

Source: AARP

MSGT DARREN THEDIECK (AIR FORCE) – BUILT OVER $600K BY AGE THIRTY-ONE

Challenge: Raised in a low-income household, Darren entered the Air Force at eighteen with a clear objective: to break the cycle of financial instability. Growing up, he watched his single mother struggle to stretch every dollar, and those early hardships ignited a passion for learning how money works. He began reading about personal finance in high school and was determined to never live paycheck to paycheck.

Strategy: As soon as Darren received his first military paycheck, he acted on his long-term wealth-building strategy. He opened a Roth IRA and a brokerage account before his twentieth birthday and began contributing consistently. He automated his savings, allocating 20% of his monthly income to investments, including his TSP. He lived far below his means, avoiding lifestyle inflation and tracking every dollar with military precision. His motto: "Treat saving like a bill you can't miss."

Darren also invested in financial education. He consumed books, followed financial influencers, and taught workshops to fellow Airmen. To multiply his impact, he created a Facebook group, "Financial Dream to Reality," where he shares tips and engages in peer mentorship with hundreds of other service members striving for similar goals.

Outcome: By the age of thirty-one, Darren's net worth exceeded $600,000, comprised of diversified holdings in index funds, retirement accounts, and cash reserves. He's well on his way to hitting his goal of $1 million in assets before age forty. Darren's consistency and discipline not only set him apart from many of his peers, but also made him a sought-after financial coach in his community. His journey is proof that wealth is not about how much you make, but how early and wisely you start managing what you earn.

Lesson: Start early, automate savings, and take full advantage of military benefits like the TSP and tax-advantaged accounts. Darren's story underscores that with discipline and education, financial independence is within reach, even on a junior enlisted salary.

Source: CNBC Make It

CAPT. NYAJUOK TONGYIK DOLUONY (ARMY) – FROM $87K IN DEBT TO OWNING HER LIFE

Challenge: Born in South Sudan, Nyajuok Tongyik Doluony spent her early life in a refugee camp before immigrating to the United States as a teenager. After escaping a forced marriage and enduring an abusive relationship, she eventually joined the U.S. Army and found purpose serving as a nurse. But life threw another challenge her way: following a serious head injury, she was deemed medically unfit for service and had to transition out of the military unexpectedly. At that time, she was a single mother of two young children and carrying a staggering $87,000 in credit card, medical, and personal loan debt. Emotionally exhausted and financially overwhelmed, Nyajuok was at rock bottom.

Strategy: With very little time before her military paychecks stopped, Nyajuok made the bold decision to confront her finances head-on. She enrolled in Dave Ramsey's Financial Peace University through her local church and dove into the principles of zero-based budgeting, the debt snowball method, and lifestyle downsizing. She created a strict budget and cut her spending to the bone—allowing herself just $100 per month for personal discretionary expenses. She sold furniture, clothes, and even family keepsakes to generate extra income. On top of her full-time job as a military nurse, she took on side gigs in healthcare—sometimes working over thirty hours on weekends alone. Her discipline and resolve allowed her to throw thousands of dollars at her debt each month.

Outcome: In less than a year, Nyajuok paid off all $87,000 in debt. She now lives in a home that she owns outright with no mortgage. Her financial stability has given her the ability to work part-time, spend more time with her children, and focus on mental and emotional healing. Empowered by her journey, she launched a nonprofit organization that helps educate and support women and children in underserved communities, both in the U.S. and abroad.

Lesson: Nyajuok's story is a testament to resilience. It proves that with determination, education, and ruthless prioritization, financial freedom is possible, even in the face of deep trauma and overwhelming odds. Her journey reminds us that your past does not define your financial future.

Source: AARP / Personal interviews

SFC DAMONE BROWN (ARMY) – FROM E-7 TO CEO

Challenge: When SFC Damone Brown transitioned out of the Army after ten years of service, he had leadership experience, logistical insight, and mission-first discipline, but he lacked business knowledge. Like many NCOs, Damone had excelled at leading troops and managing complex operations under pressure, but the civilian world of entrepreneurship was unfamiliar terrain. He faced the daunting task of translating his military background into a successful post-service career, with no roadmap and no formal education in business.

Strategy: Damone turned to the Veteran Business Outreach Center (VBOC) at Fayetteville State University, where he enrolled in their Entrepreneurial Bootcamp for Veterans (EBV). There, he learned how to write a business plan, structure operations, handle taxes, and market his services. Drawing on his Army experience in asymmetric warfare and national security, he founded Olive Drab Technologies, a consulting firm offering mission-driven solutions to clients in the defense and global security sectors. He also tapped into mentorship from experienced entrepreneurs and surrounded himself with a support network of veteran business owners to guide his early decisions.

Outcome: Today, Damone is the CEO of Olive Drab Technologies, a thriving consultancy that employs fellow veterans and military spouses. The company has secured federal contracts and built a reputation for delivering high-impact, strategic solutions with precision and integrity. Damone's leadership style reflects his military roots, and his business has become a model of veteran entrepreneurship done right. What started as an uncertain leap into the unknown has evolved into a growing enterprise with national impact.

Lesson: The same principles that drive military success, discipline, adaptability, leadership, are powerful assets in the business world. With the right guidance and resources, veterans can create impactful ventures that support both their families and their communities.

Source: Veteran Business Outreach Center Profile

This last story is one that has the most impact on me since starting this journey of educating my fellow service members and is from my perspective from getting to know Russ Smith, the 15th Master Chief Petty of the Navy.

MCPO RUSSELL SMITH (NAVY) – FROM MASTER CHIEF PETTY OFFICER OF THE NAVY TO FIRST-TIME HOMEOWNER

Challenge: After nearly forty years of service, including time as the fifteenth Master Chief Petty Officer of the Navy, Russell Smith had led thousands of Sailors through crises, global deployments, and cultural shifts within the military. Yet when it came to his own finances, he was unprepared. He'd never received formal financial training. He had no savings, no investments, and had never purchased a home. His career had been devoted to others, mentoring Sailors, representing the enlisted force, and leading from the front, but he had never taken time to plan for his own financial future.

Over a year ago, Russ joined one of my *Military, Money, and More* financial literacy classes, held virtually on Zoom. I'll never forget the moment his name popped up in the participant list. Here was a man who had seen it all, deployments, high-stakes missions, the weight of leadership, and yet, as he logged into the call, he was just another student, eager to learn. As I went through the strategies, budgeting, saving, investing, and homeownership, I noticed Russ leaning in, his camera on, his focus sharp. He wasn't just listening; he was absorbing.

I had already retired from active duty when I first met Russ. It was just after COVID struck and I had organized a Lockdown Leadership Summit through the Enlisted Leadership Foundation, held online via Zoom to provide guidance during uncertain times. As the Navy's senior enlisted leader at the time, Russ was a natural choice for an interview. I spoke with him about leading through crisis, his insights on navigating the challenges of COVID resonating deeply with our audience. His presence was commanding, his leadership undeniable, and we struck up a friendship, bonded by a mutual respect for the sacrifices of military life. Little did I know that our paths would cross again in a way that would change his future.

After the class, Russ reached out, his voice steady but passionate. "In all my thirty-seven years in the Navy," he said, "no one ever taught me this. I was so focused on the fight, I never thought about my own financial security." Russ opened up about a moment early in his career that stuck with him. As a young Weapons Technician Seaman, he bought a used car with a loan. On the lot, the price seemed fair, the payments doable, but then he saw "27.5%" next to "interest." He asked the salesman what it meant and got a casual, "That's standard for first-timers, just initial here." Trusting that, Russ signed, not fully grasping how interest worked or what it'd cost him long-term. A few days later, a trip to his ship's legal department shed light on it, but the real lesson sank in over three years of payments. That experience made him cautious, even hesitant, about financial moves like buying a home, something he didn't tackle until much later, and even then, he leaned on others for guidance.

He went further, emphasizing the urgency of the moment. "This is information that needs to be taught to every service member in the military," he told me, "especially now with the blended retirement system." There's a much larger need for our people to understand financial literacy." It was a humbling moment. Russ had climbed to the top of his profession, but like so many service members, he'd been given little guidance on how to manage his money. He'd never saved consistently. He'd never purchased a home. His focus had been on leading Sailors and serving the nation, not on building wealth or planning for life after the uniform. And yet, here he was, ready to rewrite that chapter of his story.

That conversation marked the beginning of a transformation. Russ threw himself into learning the principles we discussed in class. He started small: setting up a budget, reallocating funds to savings, and exploring his options for the future. But the real game-changer came when we began talking about homeownership. For someone who had spent decades moving from base to base, the idea of owning a home felt like a distant dream. Yet, Russ was determined to make it a reality.

Strategy: Russell joined a Military, Money, and MORE virtual financial literacy class during the COVID-19 pandemic. Despite his distinguished rank, he entered the class as a student, eager to learn and quick to engage. He absorbed the foundational strategies of budgeting, saving, investing, and homeownership. Inspired by the principles discussed, he began making changes immediately. He created a personal budget, redirected his income toward savings, and began exploring his VA loan entitlement, something he had never used. With my help and guidance through the VA loan process, he started planning for his first home purchase.

Outcome: Russell purchased his first home, a major milestone that brought a new sense of pride and permanence to his post-service life. Using the VA loan, he secured affordable financing and finally experienced the joy of owning property, something that had once felt out of reach due to a lifetime of frequent military moves. When he closed on the house, I could hear the pride in his voice. "This is mine," he told me. "For the first time, I've got something that's truly mine." Now, Russ lives with financial stability, purposefully saving, building equity, and actively mentoring younger service members. His journey had come full circle: from leading the Navy's enlisted ranks to leading by example in the realm of personal finance.

Today, Russ is applying the strategies he learned in *Military, Money, and More* with the same discipline he brought to his naval career. He's saving more, planning for retirement, and even mentoring younger Sailors about the importance of financial literacy. His story is a testament to the fact that it's never too late to take control of your financial future. No matter how far you've come or how much you've achieved, there's always room to learn, grow, and build a legacy that lasts beyond your service.

Russ's journey reminds us of a truth too many service members discover too late: financial literacy isn't just about money, it's about freedom. It's about having the tools to make choices, to live with confidence, and to create a life that reflects your values. For a man who spent nearly forty years serving others, Russ is finally serving himself; not with selfishness, but with the wisdom to secure his future. And if the fifteenth Master Chief Petty Officer of the Navy can take that step, so can you.

Lesson: No matter your rank or years of service, it's never too late to take charge of your finances. Russell's story proves that financial literacy isn't just for junior Sailors, it's essential at every level. By embracing humility and taking that first step, even the most senior leaders can secure their future and model financial readiness for the next generation. Russ's story boils down to something bigger than dollars and cents. Financial literacy, he's learned, is about freedom: freedom to choose, to live with confidence, to build something lasting. For thirty-seven years, he served others. Now, he's taking care of himself too—not out of ego, but with a quiet resolve to secure what's next. And that's a lesson worth sharing.

Source: Personal interview / Enlisted Leadership Foundation

NOTES & REFERENCES:

1. AARP. "Money Mistakes Veterans Regret." (Ericka Smith, Nyajuok Doluony)
2. CNBC Make It. "How a 31-Year-Old Air Force Tech Saved Over $600K."
3. Military.com. "The Marine Content Creator Who Outearned His Own Salary."
4. Reddit (r/Navy, r/PersonalFinance). "Financial Turnaround of a Submariner."
5. Veteran Business Outreach Center (Fayetteville State University). Profile on Damone Brown and Olive Drab Technologies.

These stories are paraphrased, not quoted directly, and are shared for educational purposes only. All individuals retain rights to their respective likeness and personal experiences.

These stories aren't just impressive—they're instructional. Whether it's climbing out of five-figure debt, reaching a six-figure net worth, or buying a first home after decades of service, each veteran's journey proves a simple truth: the mission doesn't end when the uniform comes off. It just changes.

Financial freedom isn't about perfection—it's about progress. Every decision you make today either builds your future or borrows from it. Learn from these examples. Let them be your momentum.

And remember you don't have to do it alone. If you're ready to take the next step, whether it's buying your first home, eliminating debt, or planning a career path after the military, the team at Military Operated Real Estate (MORE) is here to help.

We offer free growth seminars, homeownership counseling, and career planning resources for military families, veterans, and those who serve them. Visit www.militaryoperatedrealestate.com, call **1-888-614-MORE**, or email **admin@more-agent.com** to connect with a MORE Certified Agent or sign up for upcoming events.

You fought for this country—now let us help you own a piece of it!

I hear and forget. What I write I understand.

ABOUT THE AUTHOR

SOCIAL MEDIA

· **LinkedIn:** https://www.linkedin.com/in/traviswinfield

· **Facebook:** https://www.facebook.com/TravisWinfield

· **Instagram:** https://www.instagram.com/traviswinfield_official

· **Twitter/X:** https://twitter.com/TravisWinfield_

· **YouTube:** https://www.youtube.com/@TravisWinfield

· **TikTok:** https://www.tiktok.com/@traviswinfield

WEBSITE

Military Operated Real Estate (M.O.R.E.) Still in development